WELSH HISTORY AND ITS SOURCES

The Remaking of Wales

in the Eighteenth Century

The Remaking of Wales in the Eighteenth Century

Edited by

Trevor Herbert

Gareth Elwyn Jones

Cardiff
University of Wales Press
1988

University of Wales Press, 6 Gwennyth Street, Cathays, Cardiff CF2 4YD

© The Open University, 1988

British Library Cataloguing in Publication Data

The Remaking of Wales in the eighteenth
century.
1. Wales – 1714–1837
I. Herbert, Trevor   II. Jones, Gareth Elwyn
942.907

ISBN 0-7083-1013-3

Cover Design : Cloud Nine Design.
The publishers wish to acknowledge the advice and assistance given by the Design Department of the Welsh Books Council which is supported by the Welsh Arts Council.

Typeset by Megaron, Cardiff.

Printed in Wales by Graham Harcourt (Printers) Ltd, Swansea

Welsh History and its Sources

Welsh History and its Sources is a project conducted at the Open University in Wales from 1985 to 1988 and funded by a Welsh Office Research Development grant. The project gratefully acknowledges the financial support made available by the Secretary of State for Wales.

Project Director: Dr Trevor Herbert
Senior Visiting Fellow: Dr Gareth Elwyn Jones
Steering Committee: Mr O.E. Jones, H.M.I. (Chairman)
                          Professor R.R. Davies, History Department,
                              University College of Wales, Aberystwyth
                          Mr N. Evans, Coleg Harlech
                          Mr D. Maddox, Adviser, Mid Glamorgan LEA
                          Mr A. Evans, Head of History Department,
                              Y Pant Comprehensive School, Pontyclun

Secretary to the Project at the
Open University in Wales: Mrs Julia Williams

Contents

Illustrations

Maps and Diagrams

The Contributors

R. PAUL EVANS teaches history at Brynhyfryd School, Ruthin.

TREVOR HERBERT is Sub-Dean of Arts and Senior Lecturer in Music at the Open University, and Staff Tutor in Arts at the Open University in Wales.

BRIAN LL. JAMES is Sub-Librarian and Keeper of the Salisbury Library, University College, Cardiff.

GERAINT H. JENKINS is Senior Lecturer in Welsh History at the University College of Wales, Aberystwyth.

PHILIP JENKINS is a Lecturer in the College of Human Development at the Pennsylvania State University, USA.

GARETH ELWYN JONES is Reader in History Education at the University College of Swansea.

R.O. ROBERTS is Honorary Research Fellow at the University College of Swansea.

P.D.G. THOMAS is Professor of History at the University College of Wales, Aberystwyth.

GWYN A. WILLIAMS is Emeritus Professor of History at University College, Cardiff.

The **Debating the Evidence** sections and Glossary of this book were written by Brian Ll. James.

Preface

This series gives an insight into Welsh history by examining its sources and the ways in which some leading historians use those sources. It is not formally a history of Wales. This volume, for instance, is not a chronological history of Wales in the eighteenth century, neither is it a comprehensive history in the sense that its themes embrace all of the major issues and events that were important in that period. Readers of this book will, we hope, learn a great deal about Wales in the eighteenth century but they will learn as much about the way in which professional historians interpret the raw materials of history.

The choice of topics for the essays and the collections of documents was determined as much by the nature of the sources relevant to those topics as by the subject matter of the events or issues upon which they are based. Nevertheless, the various sections give a coherent, if not comprehensive, profile of the period. The nature of politics changed between the beginning and end of the eighteenth century, reflecting social, economic and demographic influences. Local and national government office, however, remained dominated by a landed oligarchy and it is the concerns and attitudes of these gentlemen which Philip Jenkins analyses. In Section E, Paul Evans investigates the main features of what has been called the eighteenth-century Welsh renaissance, a remarkable invention of tradition in Wales moulded from a blend of real roots and imagined splendours. Grounded more firmly in reality were the achievements of the famous preachers and teachers who infused their endeavours with single-minded missionary zeal. Geraint Jenkins sets the spectacular achievements of both *Methodism* and the *circulating schools* in a context for so long ignored by Welsh historians. Enthusiasts, in the long term, transformed Wales, but their efforts could not have been successful without both the accomplishments of their forebears and a changing society. Any history of the eighteenth century has to reflect what was to be the most profound of these changes, the industrialization of Wales, and it is to the earlier days of industrial expansion that R. O. Roberts turns. The mining of coal and the manufacture of metals were not new, but the accelerating pace of change in the later eighteenth century presaged a new Wales. To some extent, this was reflected in manifestations of a very different politics from that studied in the first section of the book. Gwyn A. Williams's account of radicalism reflects a rapidly changing Wales. It might be profitable to contemplate whether there are different ideological stances reflected in his section and Section A. Indeed, one of the purposes of the book is to open up such questions in relation to each essay and each selection of documents.

At one level, *The Remaking of Wales in the Eighteenth Century* is simply a book about the history of Wales at a time when a number of fundamental changes were taking place, and about the ways in which historians interpret that period. However, the series of which this volume is a part has been designed to serve a number of functions for anyone who is formally or informally engaged in a study of Welsh history. Those studying with a tutor, for instance extramural, university or sixth form students, will find that it is a resource which will form a basis for, or enhance, a broader study of Welsh history. Those who are studying in a more remote location, far from formal classes in Welsh history, will find that the contents of the book are so ordered as to guide them through a course of study similar, but not analogous, to the methods which have proved successful in continuing education programmes of the Open University. The main feature of this method is that it attempts to combine a programmatic approach with something more flexible and open-ended.

Central to this book are Sections A to E which contain three different but closely related and interlinked types of material. Each of the five essays is written on a clearly defined topic. Each essay is immediately followed by a collection of source material which is the basis of the evidence for the essay. Within each essay, reference is made to a particular source document by the inclusion of a reference number in the essay text; this reference number is also placed in the left-hand margin of the essay.

The sources section of each topic is followed by a section called 'Debating the Evidence'. The primary purpose here is to highlight the special features, weaknesses and strengths of each collection of sources and to question the way in which the author of the essay has used them. It is worth pointing out that we have not attempted here simply to act as *agents provocateurs*, setting up a series of artificial controversies which can be comfortably demolished. The purpose is to raise the sorts of questions which the essayists themselves probably addressed before they employed these sources. In doing this we hope to expose the types of issues that the historian has to deal with. The 'Debating the Evidence' sections pose a number of questions about the sources. They do not provide model answers and neatly tie up all of the loose ends concerning each source. The discipline of history does not allow that approach. If it did there would be no need for a book of this type. The 'Discussions' which round off each section simply put forward a number of ideas which will cause readers to consider and reconsider the issues which have been raised. The purpose is to breed the kind of healthy scepticism about historical sources which underlies the method of approach of the professional historian.

Other parts of the book support these central sections. The Introduction poses basic problems about the difficulties of coping with historical sources, points which are consolidated in the 'Debating the Evidence' sections. The intention of the opening essay, 'The Remaking of Wales in the Eighteenth Century', is to outline some of the principal changes which took place in Wales during the period and to hint at the issues that motivated these changes.

At the end of the book is a glossary which explains briefly a number of the more technical terms and concepts arising out of the Essays/Sources collections. Although a glossary is properly a list of explanations of words and terms, we have additionally included brief details of persons who are prominent in the essay and source material. Any word italicized (*thus*) will be explained in the glossary.

Readers will, of course, decide how best to profit from the different constituent elements in the book. The opening essay should certainly be read first as this provides a context for the rest of the book. It is also important to read the five essays (with or without reference to the source collections) before reading the 'Debating the Evidence' sections. It is necessary to have this broad framework for examining and re-examining the collections of sources. The 'Debating the Evidence' sections refer both forward and back to various sources on the assumption that you have familiarized yourself with the material in this way.

The open-ended nature of the book serves to highlight the extent to which it has been our intention to do no more than *contribute* to an understanding of Welsh history. Different editors would have chosen different topics. The essays here should be seen within the framework of a much wider range of writings which over the past few decades has become available. The greatest success which a book like this can meet with is that it imparts to its readers an insatiable desire to know more about Welsh history and to do so from a standpoint which is constantly and intelligently questioning the ways in which historians provide that knowledge.

Acknowledgements

The development of the Welsh History and its Sources project was made possible by the support of the Secretary of State for Wales and I am happy to have made formal acknowledgement to the Secretary of State and individuals connected with the project elsewhere in this book.

Funding from the Open University made possible the development of the initial ideas that were eventually nurtured by a Welsh Office grant. The assistance of various individuals and departments of the Open University has been frequently and freely given. In particular, I am grateful to Wynne Brindle, Richard McKracken and Barry Hollis, while my colleagues at the Open University in Wales, where the project was based, have been constantly helpful. Julia Williams, secretary to the Arts Faculty of the Open University in Wales, acted as secretary to the project. As well as word-processing the texts for the series she was immensely efficient in the administration of the project. Sandra Bewick, also of the Open University in Wales, word-processed a substantial amount of this volume with painstaking accuracy.

University College, Swansea, were kind enough to allow the part secondment of Dr Gareth Elwyn Jones to work on the project. Without him the project would not have progressed beyond being an idea as I have relied entirely on his widely respected expertise for overseeing the academic content of the series.

Diverse contributions have enhanced the effectiveness of the material. Guy Lewis, University College, Swansea, drew the maps and diagrams, often from a jumble of data and instructions. Photographic research and administration was done by Rhodri Morgan. Ceinwen Jones of the University of Wales Press copy-edited this volume and made many useful suggestions for improvement. I am grateful to Dr D.A.T. Thomas of the Open University in Wales for advice on and translation of certain Welsh-language passages.

My major debt of gratitude is to the contributors, each of whom was asked to write to a prescribed topic, format, word length and submission date. Each fulfilled the brief with absolute accuracy, punctuality and co-operation. The format was prescribed by me. Any shortcomings that remain can be put down to that prescription and to the consequences that emanated from it.

TREVOR HERBERT
Cardiff,
March 1988

Introduction

The essays contained in this book have been written not only by specialist historians, but also by specialists in the particular topic on which they have written. They are authorities on their subject and they make pertinent, informed and professional observations. Each essay is an important contribution to the historiography of Wales.

As specialists they know the sources for their topics intimately. They have included extracts from a cross-section of these sources to indicate on what evidence they base the generalizations and conclusions in their essays. We hope that the essays will interest you and that the documents will bring you into contact with the kind of primary sources which you may not have encountered before. Historians face a variety of problems when they consult source material and face even more difficulties when they have to synthesize the material collected into a coherent narrative and analysis of the events they are describing. In doing so, even the best historians make mistakes. Sometimes these are trivial (or not so trivial!) errors of fact. You may even spot factual discrepancies between information given in the various essays and the documents in this book.

At the end of each essay/sources section there is a short 'Debating the Evidence' section. By the time you reach it you will have read the essay and the sources on which the essay is based.

The 'Debating the Evidence' section is concerned with problems of interpretation. It is an attempt to conduct a debate with the author about the way in which the essay relates to the sources. This is partly achieved by asking pertinent questions about the nature of the sources. The intention is that you are stimulated to think about the validity of the exercise of writing history and the methodology of the study of history which is essentially what distinguishes it from other disciplines. The dialogue is a complex one and the questions posed do not, generally, have any 'right' answers. But they do have some answers which make more sense than others. We feel that the historians who have written the essays have provided answers which are reasonable. But historians are not infallible, however eminent they may be. Their conclusions are open to debate and discussion, as, for that matter, is their whole procedure of working. As you work through the discussion and questions you will notice that there is specific cross-referencing to the relevant section of the essay (or essays) and to sources. It is important that you use these cross-references since the success of the exercise depends vitally on taking into account the relationship between the primary source material and what the historian makes of it.

At the heart of the historian's task is the search for, and subsequent use of, evidence, much of it of the sort you will encounter here. The crucial distinction in the nature of this evidence is that between primary and secondary sources. There is no completely watertight definition of what constitutes a primary source but a reasonable working definition would be that primary sources consist of material which came into existence during the particular period which the historian is researching, while secondary sources came into existence after that period. Another important point is that the extent to which a source can be regarded as primary or secondary relies as much on the topic of research as it does on the date of that source.

This volume differs from some others in the series in that virtually all the sources are primary sources in that they emanate from the eighteenth century. You may wish to quibble that some are dated 1801, but the definition of primary and secondary sources is not a scientific rule but a useful guide. Such a guide would endorse the 'primary' classification of material written or published in 1801. This volume is also distinctive in that so much of the evidence is literary — letters, diaries or journals — as opposed to documents of record such as court proceedings. Source A.27 provides an interesting insight into the interplay of primary and secondary material. *Iolo Morganwg*'s diatribe against fox-hunters is a literary source and obviously his own opinion. It is far more in keeping with the spirit of the 1980s than the 1790s. It may represent Iolo's true sentiments, it may represent those of a wider plebeian resentment or, in theory at least, it may represent Iolo's mood at a time when he was under the influence of *laudanum*. It is still a primary source, produced about 1790. Extracts from Iolo's writings were included in G.J. Williams's book, published in 1956. It was Professor Williams's masterly scholarship which was responsible for revealing the full intricacy of Iolo's invention and forgery. It is infinitely more 'true' than much of what Iolo wrote. It is still a secondary source, being published so long after the death of Iolo. However, let us say a book were to be written called *Iolo Morganwg's Historians 1860–1960* about different reactions to Iolo throughout the nineteenth and twentieth centuries: then G.J. Williams's book would become a *primary* source.

Professor G.J. Williams is one of the best possible examples of a historian whose sources were extremely, almost impossibly, complex at times because Iolo had deliberately set out to mislead his contemporaries and posterity. While we have discussed an example of particular intricacy, the interpretation of historical sources is always extremely complex. It was once believed by highly reputable historians that if they mastered all the sources they could write 'true' history. There is at least one eminent historian who argues this now. You might like to consider on which side of the debate you stand at the moment.

Most historians would argue that this is impossible. Because we are removed from the time and place of the event, we are influenced by prejudices of nationality, religion or politics. However, there is some compensation for this because we know, usually, what the results were of actions which occurred during the period of a given topic and this benefit of hindsight is enormously useful in trying to analyse the interplay of various factors in a situation and their influence on subsequent events. As you read the essays and documents in this collection, consider the degree of objectivity and subjectivity displayed by the authors. To do this you will need to consider what you would like to know about the authors before coming to a decision and how far the authors are entitled to their own interpretations. Of course, you, too, may come to the material with your own prejudices.

There is a similar pattern of presentation for each essay and its related sources. There are specific questions involving comprehension, evaluation, interpretation and synthesis, with synthesis, arguably, the highest level of the skills. However, there can be no rigid demarcation of historical skills such as interpretation and synthesis and some questions will overlap the various categories. Neither is there a standard form of 'answer', as the discussions demonstrate. What the questions do provide is guidance for a structured pattern of study which will enhance your understanding of the essays and sources. Above all, there is dialogue and discussion about the way in which each historian has handled the complexities of writing about and interpreting the past. That such interpretation is as skilled, informed and mature as is conceivably possible is essential to our well-being as a society. In that these books are about the history of Wales they contribute fundamentally to that end. That vitality depends on debate, analytical, informed, structured debate. It is the purpose of this book to stimulate your involvement in that debate in a more structured way than has been attempted before in the study of the history of Wales.

Timechart

Wales		Other Significant Events
Birth of Griffith Jones.	**1683**	
Birth of Theophilus Evans.	**1693**	
Society for the Promotion of Christian Knowledge founded.	**1699**	
Birth of Lewis Morris.	**1701**	
	1702–13	War of Spanish Succession.
Publication of Ellis Wynne's *Gweledigaetheu y Bardd Cwsc* (*Visions of the Sleeping Bard*).	**1703**	Birth of John Wesley.
	1707	Union between England and Scotland.
	1708	Permanent charter for the Bank of England.
Death of Edward Lhuyd.	**1709**	Smelting by coke perfected by Abraham Darby.
Jacobite 'Cycle of the White Rose' started.	**1710**	
	1712	Newcomen's steam engine perfected.

Birth of Daniel Rowland. Birth of Richard Wilson (artist).	**1713**	
Birth of Howel Harris.	**1714**	Hanoverian succession. George I becomes king.
	1715	First Jacobite rebellion.
Sir Watkin Williams Wynn is Tory MP for Denbighshire.	**1716–49**	
Birth of William Williams, Pantycelyn. Publication of Theophilus Evans's *Drych y Prif Oesoedd* (*Mirror of the First Ages*).	**1716**	Septennial Act.
New issue of the Bible in Welsh.	**1717**	
	1720	South Sea Bubble.
Publication of Erasmus Saunders's *The State of the Diocese of St David's*.	**1721**	
Birth of Dr Richard Price.	**1723**	
Death of Sir Humphrey Mackworth.	**1727**	
Griffith Jones held his first school in Llanddowror.	**c.1731**	
Birth of Revd Evan Evans (Ieuan Fardd).	**1731**	
Howel Harris and Daniel Rowland join forces.	**1737**	
Birth of David Williams.	**1738**	
	1739	War of Jenkins's Ear.
	1742	Walpole resigns as Prime Minister after 21 years.

Official inception of **1743**
institutional Welsh
Methodism.

1744 First annual governing
conference of Wesleyan
Methodism.

1745 Second Jacobite rebellion.

Birth of Edward Williams **1747**
(Iolo Morganwg).

1750–70 Nearly 300 turnpike trust acts
passed.

The Honourable Society of **1751**
Cymmrodorion founded.

Isaac Wilkinson, ironmaster, **1753**
takes over Bersham works.

Birth of Thomas Charles. **1755**
Agricultural Society of
Brecknock started.

1756–63 Seven Years War.

Dowlais Iron Company **1759**
formed.
Birth of William Owen
Pughe.

Death of Griffith Jones. **1761**

John Guest and Isaac **1763**
Wilkinson lease Plymouth
ironworks.

Anthony Bacon and William **1765**
Brownrigg start ironworks at
Cyfarthfa.
Death of Lewis Morris.

Death of Theophilus Evans. **1767**

	1768	John Wilkes elected to Parliament.
	1769	James Watt patents his steam engine.
William Gilpin's tour of south Wales. Banks established in Swansea and Merthyr.	**1770**	
The Gwyneddigion first meet in London.	**1771**	
Gilpin's tour of north Wales. Death of Howel Harris.	**1773**	Boston Tea Party.
John Wilkinson patents the boring of iron cannon from solid castings.	**1774**	
	1775–83	American War of Independence.
	1776	Adam Smith's *The Wealth of Nations* published.
Richard Crawshay joins the Cyfarthfa ironworks.	**1777**	
Thomas Williams founds Parys Mine Company.	**1778**	
Death of Madam Bridget Bevan.	**1779**	
Death of Richard Wilson.	**1782**	
	1783–4	Henry Cort perfects a puddling process by which impurities could be removed from coke-smelted pig iron.
	1785	Pitt's Reform Bill defeated.

Explorer John Evans reaches the Mandan Indians.	**1786**	
Death of Ieuan Fardd.	**1788**	
	1789	French Revolution.
Death of Daniel Rowland.	**1790**	
Death of William Williams, Pantycelyn. Death of Dr Richard Price.	**1791**	Death of John Wesley.
Iolo Morganwg's first Gorsedd of the Bards Ceremony.	**1792**	Foundation of the London Corresponding Society.
Corn Riots in Wales.	**1793–1801**	
	1793–1802	French Revolutionary War.
Morgan John Rhys sails for America.	**1794**	
French landing in Fishguard.	**1797**	
	1799/1800	Combination Acts.
	1800	Act of Union between Britain and Ireland signed.
	1803–15	Napoleonic War.
Death of Thomas Charles.	**1814**	
Death of David Williams.	**1816**	
	1819	Peterloo Massacre.
Death of Iolo Morganwg.	**1826**	
Death of William Owen Pughe.	**1835**	

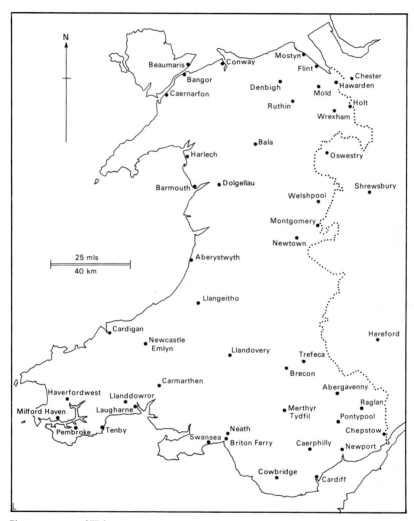

Place-name map of Wales.

The Remaking of Wales in the Eighteenth Century

PETER D.G. THOMAS

Twenty years ago or so the eighteenth century was a singularly neglected period of Welsh history. Somehow the glamorous but remote Tudor and Stuart age was transformed into a modern society recognizably similar to that of the twentieth century, without much explanation or discussion of what had happened in the mean time. There was little interest in Georgian Wales as a subject of study in its own right, apart from the *Methodist* Revival and the Industrial Revolution. Happily all that has now changed, and contributors to this volume have played a leading part in the historical renaissance. Great advances have been made in our knowledge and understanding of the period, and different interpretations of the evidence have been adopted: but if historians always agreed, history would be a dull subject.

Variations of approach can produce quite different impressions. Wales in the Georgian period could be viewed simply as a largely unchanging hierarchical society, dominated by landowners, in which every man knew his place. The first Sir Watkin Williams Wynn of Wynnstay would then be deemed the most important personality of the century, as he must have seemed to many contemporaries. For over a generation Wynn dominated the Welsh scene, to the extent of enjoying the familiar nickname of 'Prince of Wales'. His family estates ranged over half a dozen counties in north and mid-Wales, as well as over the English border. His social and political significance extended throughout the Principality, as when he was asked to intervene in the Glamorgan by-election of 1745; and on his regular visits to London he would be met outside the capital by an escort of Welsh squires, or so it is said. Yet Wynn, as a patriarch and old-fashioned *Tory*, was already an anachronistic figure, a man of the past. The future of Wales lay rather with preacher Howel Harris, educationalist Griffith Jones, radical

Robert Morris and industrialist Richard Crawshay. Therein lies the thrust of this volume, which is concerned with the political and religious, cultural and economic awakening of Wales that commenced during the eighteenth century. But first it is necessary to set the scene, to look at the Welsh society that was the background to these developments.

Georgian Wales was, of course, by modern standards, thinly peopled. In 1700 the population was around 390,000, rising to some 450,000 by 1750. These totals are estimates, calculated from the known number of births, marriages and deaths, and are based on the assumption that these had been in the same proportion as in the population of 586,000 revealed by the first official census of 1801. Even at that date the population was still evenly distributed. Glamorgan, with 70,000, had only recently overtaken Carmarthenshire as the most populous Welsh county. It was a rural society, a land of few towns; less than one-sixth of the population lived in towns. By modern standards most of them were no more than large villages. But it was a harbinger of the future that, whereas in 1700 the market town of Wrexham had been the biggest in Wales with some 3,000 inhabitants, by 1801 Merthyr Tydfil had shot into a clear lead with 7,700. Swansea just topped 6,000 in second place, but Cardiff remained at 2,000 throughout the period and was smaller than several other such local capitals as Carmarthen, Caernarfon, Denbigh and Haverfordwest.

Small as these towns were, for most Welsh people they were the centre of their life. Remoteness and isolation constitute one facet of life that still distinguished the Wales of the eighteenth century, as in earlier times, from the more modern world. Not until the reign of George III did the turnpike trusts affect significant improvement in Welsh roads, and even then not many could afford the new coach and mail services. Although we now know that mobility of population was greater than was formerly thought to be the case, it is likely that many people never left their native county throughout their lives. Instead, in a sense, the world came to them. Country folk bought clothes, hardware and other manufactures at the annual or more frequent fairs in their local market town. But it was a life of limited mental as well as physical horizons for the great majority. Wales had no newspapers of its own before Swansea's *The Cambrian* in 1804 and Bangor's *North Wales Chronicle* in 1808. Although the weekly papers of the English border towns circulated widely in Wales (and, incidentally, form a much neglected source of Welsh history for the period), their readership must have been limited to the gentry, lawyers, clergy and merchants. Lesser folk would glean news of the wider world from their betters, pub gossip, and from the travelling pedlars who made regular visits to the villages.

Even more remarkable to modern eyes than this sense of isolation was the vast social and economic gulf between the classes. While labourers earned less than £10 a year, their local village squire would enjoy an annual income of £500 to £1,000. In between there were tenant farmers and *freeholders* working their own land: but a significant gap existed between these men, barely able to maintain themselves in modest self-sufficiency, and the gentry. It was the divide between the working and the leisured classes. For the hired labourers and small farmers, social life revolved around the village community, with, in most cases, the squire a benevolent despot, a role supplemented by that of the parson, for the Church was the dispenser of charity as well as religion. During much of this period it was still customary for many parishes to maintain their own paupers, especially in the more remote areas, with the money for this coming from a variety of charitable and other sources and being administered by the vicars.

Contemporary urban life qualifies this traditional picture of a sharply divided society. In the towns, although there did not yet exist to any great extent a business or entrepreneurial class, there were by now a number of 'middling folk', men who derived incomes from professional work and administrative employment. Among them may be numbered the clergy, customs officials and other government men, lawyers and a handful of doctors and schoolmasters. These men earned more than labourers and artisans, but not many above £100 a year, well below the income of most squires. Although this embryonic middle class was another portent of the future, Georgian Wales was ruled in every sense by the landowners.

The squires, the great men of their village, were the gentry of the county, numbering perhaps between 25 and 50 in each shire, with landed incomes of £500 and upwards. They met regularly during the year in their county town, and many came to acquire houses there. They formed the county society of Wales. But there was a clear distinction within the gentry stratum itself between those who were MPs and those who were merely JPs. Several hundred Welsh squires would be JPs at any one time, but there were only 27 Welsh MPs. A small number of leading families, perhaps 30 to 40 altogether in the whole of Wales, controlled and contested the Parliamentary representation. These top families of

Wales, some of whom obtained peerages, formed an oligarchy, with incomes from £3,000 to £5,000 and above. Membership of the House of Commons was valued not merely for prestige but also as the way to control local government and patronage. The shire member might himself become *Custos Rotulorum* and therefore chairman of the *county Bench*, and could also hold the more honorific office of Lord-Lieutenant. He would claim the right to nominate to the bench and to official appointments in his area, a claim usually conceded unless he was much out of favour with the government in London. Such potential rewards led the powerful families now to exclude from Parliament the lesser squires who had had their turn in Tudor and Stuart times. These gentlemen, with only a dozen or a score of voters at their command, could not aspire to compete with *magnates* whose 'interest' in a county might comprise a hundred voters. Nor was there much chance of the smaller squires or new men breaking into the privileged circle. No new blocks of land were available to found estates, such as had come in earlier centuries from Crown, Church and civil wars. Oligarchy, in Wales as elsewhere in Britain, became ever more entrenched, by such devices as the entail of estates and the marriage of heirs with heiresses.

Another characteristic of Georgian Wales remarkable to modern eyes was the freedom from control by the central government. The eighteenth century was virtually an era of home rule in Wales, albeit rule by the squires. The Glorious Revolution of 1688 marked the triumph of the gentry over the Crown. With the final abolition of the royal prerogative courts there was no effective supervision over the local government of Wales through the Quarter Sessions, which formed not only the judiciary but in many ways also the legislature and the executive of each county. Quarter Sessions came to impose highway rates, poor rates, and occasional general taxes to raise money needed by the county to maintain bridges, the shire hall or the gaol. Magistrates also had some control over the local economy by their regulation of weights and measures, prices and wages.

This then was the golden age of the gentry in society, in government, and also in politics. Parliamentary elections were usually uncontested, for in both county and borough constituencies the overwhelming majority of the Welsh parliamentary electorate, some 25,000 in 26 constituencies, were dependants of the gentry, directly as tenants and leaseholders or indirectly as tradesmen, innkeepers and others desirous of the squire's goodwill. But as yet the factor of coercion was less important than the sense of loyalty to the local squire, and the candidate he supported. Undue pressure was not needed at a time when political consciousness was undeveloped among the great mass of the population. Spontaneous reactions to national events were rare even among the gentry. Residual sympathy for the former royal house of Stuart manifested itself in *Jacobitism*, but that was never a popular movement. The embodiment of that sentiment in such gentry organizations as the Cycle of the White Rose and the Society of Sea Serjeants owed more to masculine clubbability and the contemporary fashion for secret societies than to political fervour, as the subsequent development of widespread *freemasonry* was to demonstrate.

Even in quiet Hanoverian Britain, Wales was renowned, or notorious, for its political torpor. Welshmen who wanted to change the world made for London: men like Robert Morris, founding Secretary of the Bill of Rights Society, and the radical MP Sir Watkin Lewes; and those famous men of word rather than deed, *Richard Price* and *David Williams*. But Wales itself took long to stir. No petition of protest was sent up to London against the treatment of *John Wilkes* in the 1760s. On the outbreak of the War of American Independence in 1775 only three petitions from Wales, totalling some 500 signatures, were directed to the Crown. All were in favour of government policy! Their geographical distribution (Carmarthenshire, Carmarthen and Haverfordwest) points to the guiding hand of George Rice, the Carmarthenshire MP who was a leading ministerial spokesman on America and who doubtless wished to demonstrate the support of his home area. So-called public opinion was still a political weapon of the gentry. The political awakening of Wales in a modern sense was a plant of late growth. Not until the 1780s were the first challenges made to the rule of local oligarchs in such counties as Flintshire and Glamorgan.

Such a backward and conservative society would not seem to constitute a promising seed-bed for the variety of changes that form the theme of this volume. But it was this very circumstance of quiescence, in many respects a deteriorating situation of abuse and decline, that both provided the opportunity for a religious revival and proved the incentive for a deliberate recovery, or creation, of national consciousness. Moreover, as is apparent from the papers in this volume, most of the influences that helped to transform Wales were not indigenous, but came from outside: the *Methodist* Movement, the *French Revolution*, the Romantic Movement, and the Industrial Revolution.

It should be apparent, also, that the above brief sketch of Georgian Wales has necessarily been painted with too broad a brush. A hierarchical society it may have been, but not one rigidly tiered into classes of labourers, small farmers, lesser squires and landed *magnates*, for there were infinite gradations of income and status. The dominating class of landowners was not homogeneous in any respect, ranging from *freeholders* who proudly styled themselves 'esquire' to wealthy aristocrats. In many parts of Wales the gentry, especially those in the higher ranks, were becoming increasingly absentee, anglicized, and alienated from the mass of a population that remained 90 per cent Welsh-speaking. In his recent study of the Glamorgan gentry, Philip Jenkins comes near to depicting a rural situation more analogous to Ireland than England. Yet both in that county and elsewhere many squires took a prominent role in the economic development of their localities, if only to supplement their landed incomes. They were not all idle and bucolic! And, in any case, industrialization and agricultural improvement had commenced in Wales long before *George I* came to the throne in 1714.

The seventeenth century had witnessed so many political and religious upheavals that people, high and low, were only too thankful for a time of peace and quiet. It is easy now to forget that in 1700 Britain's recent political record caused her to be seen as the most unstable country in Europe. A deferential society was in part a natural reaction, with a respect for convention and authority in all classes: 'the moral economy of the crowd' depicted by E.P. Thompson was an acceptance of the constraints of law and property tempered by the dire necessity of hunger. But Britain's recent history had nevertheless bequeathed a legacy, not merely of political memory and tradition but also of religious minorities, dissenting congregations already outside the established Church and numbering perhaps 10 per cent of the Welsh population. In various ways economic, religious and political changes had already commenced long before the developments discussed in this volume.

History is said to be written by the winners. Certainly it is difficult to see much of the life of Georgian Wales except from the viewpoint of the landowners. For the bulk of our information comes from their family papers; from the records of the administrative and judicial institutions that they managed; and from the literature that they read. One contributor to this volume, Philip Jenkins, goes so far as to claim that it is not possible to write a political history of the lower classes in this period because so little is known of their opinions. Certainly it is the gentry of Glamorgan and of south-west Wales that have been the subjects of stimulating recent studies by, respectively, Jenkins and David Howell. The eighteenth century suffers from a dearth of information compared with more modern times, both altogether and more especially in a statistical sense. Wise historians of the period qualify their conclusions and make frequent confessions of ignorance. It is virtually impossible to ascertain (even more so than nowadays) how genuinely spontaneous were manifestations of public opinion. Economic historians necessarily dispute the respective weight to be attached to the various causes of the Industrial Revolution. And, as is made evident here by Paul Evans, historians of the 'Welsh Renaissance' even encounter problems of forgery, falsehood and fantasy created by patriotic fervour. Least obvious, and most difficult, is the problem of penetrating the contemporary mind. Acceptance of one's place in the hierarchical society of the time was a contemporary phenomenon that needs to be explained rather than criticized. These stimulating papers and their documentation should provide much food for thought on these problems.

Political Quiescence and Political Ferment

PHILIP JENKINS

The eighteenth century in Wales was a period of dramatic developments in industrial history, as well as momentous changes in religion and education. Before the 1770s, however, Welsh politics can appear rather dry and uneventful. There is little to compare with the events of the *Civil War* era on the one hand, or the *Chartist* and *Rebecca* movements on the other. Welsh politics, for most of the eighteenth century, appears to have been the preserve of a handful of wealthy landowners, who browbeat their poor tenants into appearing at the hustings once every few years.

While the great lords and squires undoubtedly did exist, and were powerful, a picture of graveyard tranquillity is grossly exaggerated. Wales in this period had a turbulent political life, the issues of which combined both the unresolved debates of the seventeenth century and (in some measure) the newer politics of the industrial era. The political history is worth studying for its own intrinsic interest, but also because it provides an essential framework without which neither economic nor religious developments can be properly understood.

PARLIAMENT

In eighteenth-century Wales, most counties had a straightforward constituency organization, with one member each for the county and the borough. The exceptions were Merioneth (only one member in all), Monmouthshire and Pembrokeshire (three members each). Together, Wales and Monmouthshire had a total of twenty-seven parliamentary representatives — roughly one MP for every 15,000 of the population.

Freeholders elected the county member. A borough MP was chosen by the *burgesses* of all the towns eligible to participate in the election, and that number changed somewhat during the century. In Montgomeryshire, for example, the *'out-boroughs'* were disfranchised in 1728 — and that was taken to include every borough except Montgomery. Such decisions as these — and others concerning the election of members — were taken by Parliamentary committees which regularly and unashamedly exercised their power in blatantly partisan ways.

At a lower level, the franchise was subject to considerable partisan manipulation. If a *magnate* controlled a borough, he might well succeed in extending the status of *burgess* to his friends and followers (A.1). Even at the county level — an open and relatively 'democratic' arena — partisan *sheriffs* would often disqualify opponents. In Glamorgan in 1745, some 1,500 men voted, representing perhaps 10 or 15 per cent of the adult male population — by contemporary standards, a very respectable turn-out. The first ballot gave the *Tory* candidate a healthy majority of 200. After the *Whig sheriff* had done his worst, this was converted to a 50-vote margin for his *Whig* ally.

With such factors at work, it will be obvious that eighteenth-century Wales was very far from parliamentary democracy in any modern sense. The individual vote might count a great deal, but only in certain circumstances. Moreover, the choice of candidates from which a voter could pick was extremely limited. All were either members of the traditional landed élite, or up-and-coming Court servants currently attempting to enter that circle.

The ideal election was one in which a candidate was returned without having divided his community, so formal opposition was discouraged by the ethos of the landed classes (A.2). The landowners held a meeting to assess the claims of those most anxious to serve in Parliament, and tried to achieve a reasonable balance (A.3). These agreements were regarded as morally binding, even when they resulted in a bitterly divided county like Anglesey uniting to elect a 'consensus' county member (A.4, A.5). In such a case, the election was a formality. This was

A.1

A.2

A.3

A.4

A.5   less an intentional conspiracy against the electorate than a pressing attempt to reduce the horrific expense caused by
A.6   contested elections (A.6). Naturally, electors were expected to follow the orders of their landlords, though reprisals were
A.7   rarely as indiscriminate as in Victorian Wales (though see A.7).

One of the most difficult points for a twentieth-century person to grasp about Georgian society is the extremely narrow nature of formal political representation. Wales had few seats, and elections were infrequent. The time between elections was lengthened from three to seven years in 1716. There were only rare opportunities to enter parliamentary politics, even for landed families.

In Glamorgan, for example, there were roughly 90 to 100 families with some claim to gentility or gentry status at any point during the eighteenth century. Oversimplifying greatly, let us suppose that there were, during the whole century, some 400 men who were heads of gentry families (it goes without saying that political representation was a male preserve, though women often played a vital but informal role in the electoral process). Between 1700 and 1800, Glamorgan was represented by only 23 individuals for county and borough combined. Two *Mackworths*, father and son, hogged the borough seat from 1739 to 1790. Parliamentary representation, therefore, was not even a matter to be decided within the ranks of the landed class as a whole. It was a prospect only for the élite, the leading ten or twenty families within a county.

There is no question that the landed oligarchy dominated parliamentary constituencies. Counties differed chiefly in whether they had only one overwhelming 'Leviathan', or if there were enough powerful families to provide lively competition. Some constituencies appear to have become almost hereditary possessions, especially for a family like the Williams Wynns of Denbighshire. The first Sir Watkin Williams Wynn inherited vast estates in Denbighshire, Shropshire and Caernarfonshire on his father's death in 1740. He served as Denbighshire's parliamentary representative from 1716 to 1741, and again from 1742 until his death in 1749. His son (another Sir Watkin) was an infant in 1749, but he grew up to represent the county from 1774 to 1789. The third Sir Watkin was MP from

Sir Watkin Williams Wynn: a portrait by Thomas Hudson, 1740. (*Source: National Museum of Wales.*)

1796 to 1840. A similar tale could be told in most counties, as with the Morgan family of Monmouthshire.

It looks almost as though political power was a matter of right for the owner of a wealthy estate, a debt owed to him by society, and an affair in which political issues played little or no part. This would be far from the truth — as would the obvious consequence of such a view, that real political life was all but dead in Georgian Wales. Parliament was one aspect of politics — admittedly very important, but by no means the only one. Welsh constituencies were simply too few, and potential claimants too numerous, for every contest to be fought to the death. In the eighteenth century, therefore, party contests were often fought at many lower levels: in the boroughs, the *county Bench*, the *lieutenancy*, and above all in the battles for patronage in Church, army, universities, even in local grammar schools (A.13).

A.13

These struggles raged far outside the charmed circle of county society, with key activists including many 'new men' — attorneys, industrialists, borough notables and clergymen. Party conflict even shaped the emergence of Welsh industry, with high *Tory* landowners naturally preferring entrepreneurs of like mind in the exploitation of their estates. In no period of British history has the apparent tranquillity of 'high' politics been so far removed from the rich ferment in the localities.

PARTY POLITICS

It cannot be sufficiently emphasized that in eighteenth-century Wales, there were deeply held partisan political views, which caused violent conflicts at many levels of society. Politics could kill — in riots, or in *treason trials*. Naturally, much of the very sensitive political correspondence of the time no longer survives, but there is enough to show that conspiracy, threats of insurrection or invasion and negotiations with hostile powers, were all reasonably familiar phenomena in eighteenth-century Wales. We can still find correspondence ending with what must have been a familiar refrain — 'Burn this letter!'

Of course, by no means all party loyalists even dabbled in such extremism; but the question remains, if parliamentary affairs were so relatively static, what were people fighting about? To understand this, we must appreciate the complex and closely intertwined relationship between religion, social structure and history. Traditionally, the landed élite controlled the localities, unchallenged by rival groups ever since the *Reformation* had both tamed and impoverished the Church. The Church was an arm of the state, while in turn religious

A.8   conformity was required of secular office-holders (A.8). In the seventeenth century, there had been a series of threats to the status quo, emanating from an over-ambitious central government under the perceived influence of religious extremists — *Laudian High Churchmen* in the 1630s, *Puritans* in the 1650s, *Roman Catholics* in the 1680s. In each case, religious dogmatism was intimately connected with a threat to the local power of the landowners, above all in key administrative offices like *Deputy-Lieutenant* and *Justice of the Peace*. In Wales, this had been further complicated by the identification of the *Catholic* presence (especially strong in Monmouthshire) with the threat of Irish invasion.

By about 1700, there were two major parties, *Whig* and *Tory*. Each had its characteristic ideas and — even more important — each had a stereotype of its rival. The central disagreement in the whole conflict was the nature of the perceived threat to social order and local autonomy. The *Tories* upheld the Church interest and opposed the toleration of *Dissenters*, who were after

A.9–   all the heirs of the *Roundheads* (A.9–A.11). To the cry that
A.11   *Dissenters* were 'fellow Protestants', some responded with
A.12   sentiments considerably less than ecumenical (A.12). *Dissenters* were also numerous — perhaps 10 per cent of the Welsh population in 1720 — and their sheer numbers seemed

A.13   threatening to Church loyalists (A.13). Throughout the century, high Anglican opinions were kept alive, at least in part, by the annual celebration of the feast of King Charles the Martyr.

In the *Tory* view, the *Whigs* were corrupt hypocrites who threatened to ruin the gentry by excessive taxes. For most of the century, the *Tories* also represented the old 'Country' tradition of regional opposition to virtually all government, especially if it cost anything.

For the *Whigs*, by contrast, the true threat lay in the dictatorial and crypto-*Catholic* tendencies of the *Tories*, successors to the Royalist adventurers of the 1640s and James II's *Papist* Court. The *Catholicism* and tyranny that *Tories* would introduce meant mass impoverishment — reduction to 'wooden shoes' on the

A.14 French model (A.14). *Dissenters* were at worst misled brethren, at best useful allies in the struggle for popular education and evangelization.

Roman Catholics were seen by *Whigs* as a real menace, especially in Monmouthshire, where they were a conspicuous presence. There were probably some 800 *Catholics* here in the early part of the century, some 2 per cent of the county population. Conflict and persecution continued well into mid-century. In the 1750s, even the son of a prominent *recusant* family was warned to be discreet in the practice of his faith, lest

A.15 he outrage local *Whigs* (A.15).

Contemporary political struggles were seen very much in religious, even mystical, terms, with divine portents foretelling

A.16 the downfall of a *Catholic* tyrant like *Louis XIV* (A.16). Even in the much more secular atmosphere of the 1750s, there were many in Wales who saw the commercial war against France as an apocalyptic struggle. It would be very rash to attempt to draw a line between religion and politics in such a society.

History, equally, was a vital element of political conflict, which was often fought out through polemical accounts of recent history, especially focusing on the *Civil War* years. In the early eighteenth century, both Anglicans and Nonconformists attempted to collect accounts of the misdeeds of the other's enemies. In 1709, Glamorgan Anglicans even claimed that their antiquarian efforts were thwarted by *Whig* followers of the

A.17 Nonconformist scholar, *Edmund Calamy* (A.17). Little, it seemed, could be politically neutral in such an atmosphere.

From the 1690s, the ideological fight merged into a very practical struggle for economic advantage, indeed survival, with the great increase in government patronage. Controlling government meant the ability to help and reward supporters, and to exclude enemies from essential local offices. Purges of rivals reached a height between about 1708 and 1722, and the records provide an excellent guide to local political loyalties. For example, in 1714, Lord Chancellor Harcourt was adding loyal

A.18

Tories to *county Benches* as fast as he was removing die-hard *Whigs*; in 1715 the *Whig* Lord Cowper returned the favour (A.18).

Already by 1710, there was an economic content to political rivalry; and this grew rapidly during the wars of the next half-century. *Whigs* tended to support land wars in Europe, paid for by land taxes which were desperately unpopular among the gentry. *Tories* supported naval wars, involving privateering and the grabbing of colonies. This was very much in the interests of Bristol and Liverpool — and of both landowners and industrialists in those Welsh counties which formed part of the metropolitan areas of those great ports. In the 1730s, therefore, Welsh *Tories* became increasingly desperate as Walpole's

A.19 government seemed to fulfil all their worst fears (A.19).

But it was in the first quarter of the century that the crisis was at its deepest, and had its greatest impact on everyday life — in the selection of one's patrons and friends, the books one read and the clubs patronized, even taste in drink (claret was French and *Tory*; port was *Whiggish*). In addition to the running religious debate, there was the new and appallingly divisive issue of the succession. Would Queen Anne be followed by her brother, the *Catholic 'James III'*, or by a Protestant relative, *George of Hanover*? In hindsight, we know that the Hanoverian cause triumphed in 1714, but only a fool would have seen this as an easy or natural outcome at the time. The *Jacobite* view was very widely held in Wales, with the consequence that *Whig* governments found themselves appointing local officials to attempt to control deeply disaffected localities.

If we are to believe local *Whigs*, the area between Machynlleth and Aberystwyth was in a particularly parlous state by 1720. Squires openly drank treasonable healths; their agents interfered with the mails; they ran an escape network for fugitives and army deserters; and they corresponded with the exiled *Jacobite* court (this last is unquestionably true). Meanwhile, government supporters were persecuted, and the few *Whig* landowners in the area were calling for the stationing of regular troops to prevent traitors from winning the next

A.20 election (A.20).

In turn, local *Tories* had cause to fear implication in one of a number of conspiracies, real or invented. In 1723, *Robert Mansell*

of Glamorgan suggested that after the '*Atterbury plot*,' any *Tory*
A.21   leader might find himself involved in a 'show trial' (A.21).

During the 1720s, fears of an actual *Jacobite* coup or invasion
began to be dispelled, but the high *Tory* gentry were scarcely
reconciled to the government. In Wales, this disaffection was
manifested in the form of new party clubs and organizations,
like the 'Cycle in the North', or the 'Sea Serjeants' in the south
A.22   and west (A.22). These societies acted as a form of *Tory* party
organization, together (no doubt) with some flirting with
conspiracy and treasonous correspondence. Much of it may
have been rhetoric, but some may not. When a new *Jacobite*
invasion did occur in 1745, most of the leading *Tories* rallied to
the government against what was seen as a bizarre adventure.
Some, however, did not — and a few documents preserve their
A.23   views (A.23). There were also a handful who put their beliefs
into practice, with predictable results — the gallows for
Glamorgan's David Morgan, exile for the Monmouthshire
Vaughans.

Even when such an immediate crisis was lacking, party
politics continued to have a vigour — we might say, savagery
— that could not be guessed from the staid history of
constituencies. In the borough of Carmarthen, for example,
political divisions often erupted into violence in the century
after 1740, though the factional labels changed. Between 1740
and 1760, the Sea Serjeants were a leading force, from their
party headquarters in the Red Lion Inn. In 1755, there were
appalling riots which earned the attention of the London press
— not least because the street fights had apparently graduated
A.24   from cudgels and knives to the use of naval cannon (A.24).

Of course, it may well be questioned how far genuine
questions of ideology, still less religion, motivated such people
— or the rioters who assaulted Dissenting meeting-houses in
the last years of Queen Anne. However, party labels did have
their appeal, especially at times of the deepest economic
depression — in 1710, 1740, 1766 or 1795. During such crises,
labels like '*Jacobite*' were useful badges at once designed to focus
communal loyalty and outrage one's social betters.

Traditional *Whig* and *Tory* rhetoric would continue to
be heard until the very end of the century. Indeed, some

anti-*Methodist* writers in the age of *Thomas Charles* would continue to act as though *Oliver Cromwell* was a very recently deceased figure. However, matters were changing. In the 1760s, Country and radical views were increasingly detached from the Tory party as the county *magnates* returned to their natural role of conservative upholders of the state as presently constituted. The new radicals built their cause on very modern issues — *Wilkes*, the nationalist struggles in America and Ireland — but they drew on old roots. The old *Jacobite* clubs were now transformed into more secular, radical groupings, usually under the title of *freemasonry* (at Carmarthen, the new Masonic lodge was founded at the Red Lion Inn, just as the 'Sea Serjeants' club there was becoming moribund).

In the 1770s and 1780s, Wales entered a period of new political alignments — not yet the class struggles of the Industrial Revolution, but still something different from the old conflicts deriving from the *Civil War*. And these new conflicts proved a training ground for many of the later radicals — *Richard Price* and *Iolo Morganwg*, among many others. The new reformers represented a striking coalition of gentry and industrialists (often former *Tories* or *Jacobites*) together with liberal *Dissenters* and not a few pure adventurers. Although not a united party in any modern sense, they tended to call for a common body of reforms: in the structure of borough government, reform of inept oligarchies; in the theology of the established Church, moves towards 'liberal' (often *Unitarian*) views; and protests against the Church's monopoly of religious life. The rhetoric of these reformers can broadly be described as populist rather than revolutionary, but it merged easily with the whirlwind of new ideas that accompanied the *French Revolution*.

In terms of parliamentary politics, the reformers allied to provide effective support in a series of elections in the 1780s. Although the candidates they supported were still very traditional landowners, the rhetoric of the campaigns was very different: populist, anti-aristocratic, and pro-religious toleration (A.25, A.26). In Pembrokeshire in 1780 and Glamorgan in 1789, the 'Independent' campaigns have left some fascinating records. In contemporary Carmarthen, borough attacks on the

A.25
A.26

Pembroke town and castle, painted by Richard Wilson. (Source: National Museum of Wales.)

Bishop of St Davids led to a very striking development, a campaign based on considerable *anticlericalism*.

The long reign of George III saw dramatic changes in Welsh politics — from 'traditional' *Whig* and *Tory*, through the populist 'new politics,' and finally to overt class politics, in which new classes laid their claim to a political voice. It was a time of change — by no means simply the torpid and quiescent Wales of Victorian legend.

It might justly be remarked that in one area at least, such a legend seems close to reality. It is all but impossible to write a political history of the lower classes in eighteenth-century Wales, because they have left so few records of their own opinions. The political élite apparently viewed the plebeians as little better than useful dupes; in turn, the poor responded with a generalized class resentment that too seldom finds written

A.27   commemoration (but see A.27). Concerted plebeian political action is difficult to trace before the 1750s, though we then begin to find effective protests against what were seen as

A.28   artificially generated food scarcities (A.28, A.29).

A.29   About 1760, Sir Charles Hanbury Williams of Pontypool commented on the pathetic spectacle of an old labouring man

A.30   asserting his Royalist and *Tory* sentiments (A.30). After 1790, the propertied and respectable would often have cause to look back nostalgically to such an obsequious age; for a new industrial order was shortly to challenge traditional political structures.

Sources

A.1   [This petition] sheweth that Sir Arthur Owen, baronet, with an intent to gain the government of the said borough of Pembroke wholly into his own hands, in the year 1704 procured himself to be elected a mayor of the said town of Pembroke, although by the charters of the said borough of Pembroke he was not qualified so to be, and by reason of the said election and some pretended new election continued to serve the said office of mayor for two years successively although he was not (as your petitioners are advised) legally admitted thereunto, during which time the said Sir Arthur Owen admitted and swore great numbers of his dependants, tenants and servants who did not live within the liberties of the said borough of Pembroke, to be common councilmen and *burgesses* of the said borough, contrary to the charters and bye-laws of the said borough, thereby intending to bring the election of *burgesses* to serve in Parliament for the said borough and the return thereof wholly into his own power, and deprive your petitioners as well as the other legal electors of their rights of election or having any share therein.

(Petition to Parliament, *c.*1710, from the Mayor and burgesses of Wiston, Pembs. National Library of Wales, Bronwydd MS 1674.)

A.2   [I am] sorry you persist in occasioning a contested election in Carmarthenshire when you always knew that I could not be for you this time. There can be nothing so agreeable to me as to see the county quiet and unanimous, therefore I shall take it as a particular favour if you will accommodate this matter with Mr Rice.

(Letter of the Duke of Bolton to Sir Nicholas Williams, 5 March 1722. National Library of Wales, Edwinsford MS 2907.)

A.3   At the election at Monmouth in 1696 [*recte* 1695?] you and my cousin Morgan served for *knights*, and I served for *burgess* of Monmouth, and you promised you would resign the next turn to Sir John Williams, now chosen for the county; and Probert for the town; and then all those promised that the next parliament, you should be *knight* and I should be *burgess*. This Mr Morgan and several others owned again and again, and cannot be denied.

(Letter of John Arnold to Sir Charles Kemys, 10 January 1700. National Library of Wales, Kemys-Tynte MSS.)

A.4   St James's Street
December 6th 1744

Dear Sir,
   I have been desired to send you the following proposal from

Mr Edwin, which has already been offered to the Duke of Beaufort, and to which his Grace will give no answer.

Mr Edwin consents to give you his Interest at the present election upon these conditions. He fully intends to cultivate his interest and offer himself as a candidate at the next election for Westminster, but in case he should not be chosen there, he expects that the Duke of Beaufort, Lord Windsor, Lord Mansell and the rest of your friends in Glamorganshire will engage to give him their interest at the next general election for that county.

These are Mr Edwin's conditions, and as I have promised to transmit them to you, you will excuse me, and send your answer the first opportunity to
Dear Sir Charles
Your most obliged
and faithful servant
Thomas Prowse.
Pray send your answer to no one but me.

(Letter to Sir Charles Kemys-Tynte. Glamorgan Record Office, D/D, KT/1/27.)

A.5 . . . about 9 o'clock, all the Gentlemen from Carnarvanshire and this County mett at ye house of Mr David Wms an Attorney . . . where the Candidate [Mr Bayly] lay . . . at which place they staid till half an hour past ten, when My Lord Bulkeley, with several other Gentlemen that had lain the night before at Baronhill came . . . then they all proceeded to ye County Hall, and ye King's writt being read, and the Act of Parliament against Bribery and Corruption read likewise, they proceeded to Elect. When Ld. Bulkeley Polled for Mr Baily, Mr Meyrick, Mr Bodvell etc. did ye same, after which all ye house catched ye word, and there was nothing heard but Baily, Baily, Baily without intermission, till they were tired ecchoing the name, after which the Sherriff declared him duely elected (Proclamation being made before, that if anybody did demand a Pole for anybody else they should appear, but nobody did) the Elected Member with all the Electors, dined at the Bull's Head Inn, where a grand Entertainment was made 3 Barrels of Ale were given the Populace at the Cross to drink.

(Diary of William Bulkeley of Brynddu, Anglesey, May 9, 1734. Quoted in G. Nesta Evans, *Religion and Politics in Mid-Eighteenth Century Anglesey*, Cardiff, 1953, pp.138–9.)

A.6 This sudden accident will probably cause much alterations in that County, as this Gentleman had at a prodigious expence maintained his Interest in that County for above 30 years against Chirk Castle Family backed with all the power and influence of the Court aided with the resources of ye Treasury, by which he plunged a Estate of 15000 pounds a year to 120000 pounds in debt.

(Ibid., p.138, on the death of Sir Watkin Williams Wynn, 1749.)

A.7 To The Right Hon'ble Thomas Lord Mansel of Margam,
These humbly present
My Lord,
Upon several threatening Expressions of one of your understewards in these parts to dispossess me of the lands I have held under your noble family for threescore years last past and this too to be done without any just occasion and as I conceive without your Lordships knowledge, I humbly beg Leave to Lay my case open to your Lordship, that it may better appear what injustice is like to be done one of your Oldest Tenants for doing what it was not in my power to help. My fault is, voting in the last Election for your cousin Jones of Buckland, a thing I always refused to do until forced to it by the frequent and personal solicitations of my other landlord Mr Morgan of Tredegar who (besides his agents) was with me no less than four times to press me to give my vote, and still denied until he Assured that your Lordship would not be angry and at Last was carried up to the court betwixt him and his brother. I hope, My Lord, that I have not in this case transgressed beyond all hopes of pardon for I do assure your Lordship had both my Landlords appeared in person I should not have failed to choose your Lordship but being attacked so violently by Mr Morgan and your Lordship being at too great a distance to defend me I could not resist. My

Lord, I shall not trouble your Lordship with anything more upon this occasion but that my wife and I are so old as betwixt us to make nearly 160 years and pray that your Lordship would not remove us at this great age.
I am
My good Lord
Your most obliged Tenant
and humble servt.
John Watkin.
Cevenbrynych.
May ye 8th 1722.

(National Library of Wales, Penrice and Margam MS L1014.)

A.8   We Rice Pierce, minister of the parish and parish church of Llangelynin in the county aforesaid, and John Owen and Edward Alban, churchwardens of the same parish, do hereby certify that Hugh Thomas of Hendre, esquire, present high *sheriff* of the county aforesaid, did upon the Lord's day commonly called Sunday, (namely) the first day of April last past in the parish church of Llangelynin aforesaid, immediately after divine service and sermon, receive the sacrament of the Lord's Supper according to the usage of the Church of England. In witness whereof we have hereunto subscribed our hands the eighth day of April in the year of our Lord 1733.
Rice Pierce, rector of Llangelynin.
John Owen.
Edward E. Alban.

(Sacrament certificate in Merionethshire Quarter Sessions roll, quoted in Keith Williams-Jones, *Calendar of the Merionethshire Quarter Sessions Rolls*, Merioneth County Council, 1965, Vol.I, p.5.)

A.9   [Your new title is] an earnest of greater honours, well deserved by your Lordship and your ancestors. The signalising conduct in our late deliverance out of the management of wicked and rebellious principled men will be to your Lordship's immortal glory.

(Letter of Alexander Purcell, Cardiff, to Lord Mansell, Margam, [1] January 1711. National Library of Wales, Penrice and Margam MS L718.)

A.10   If it be about any preferment, take this caution, that My Lord will have nothing to do with anybody that depends on Sir Peter [King] (and God be praised). Sir Peter, nor no *Whig* or Fanatic, are in reputation here, times are altered.

(Letter of Edward Mansell of Henllys (Gower) to William Lucas, 3 March 1712. National Library of Wales, Penrice and Margam MS L729.)

A.11   When they [the *Dissenters*] had the reins of government in their hands, in former times, what havoc and devastation, what sacrilege and cruelty etc. were committed throughout the land! And who knows but the same restless factious spirit still lurks in the dark, and only waits a fit opportunity of breaking out, with redoubled force unto all manner of outrage and rebellion from which, Good Lord, deliver us!

(Sermon of Revd Thomas Davies of Coity, Glamorgan, March 1790. Glamorgan Record Office, D/D, SR/16/72.)

A.12   And these fanatic saints, though neither in
Doctrine or discipline our brethren,
Are fellow Protestants and Christians
As much as Hebrews or Philistines.
But in no other sense than Nature
Hath made a rat our fellow creature.
Lice from a body suck their food,
But is a louse our flesh and blood?

(Letter of Henry Moore to George Wynne of Leeswood, Flintshire, *c*.1733. National Library of Wales, Leeswood MS 1992.)

A.13   But I am sorry I must acquaint your Lordship that above three-fourths of the abovementioned inhabitants are *Presbyterians* professing themselves for the most part *Arminians*, with a few

Calvinists and fewer *Anabaptists*, and among all these I am afraid are too many *Deists*.

(Letter of Thomas Price, rector of Merthyr Tydfil, in response to the 1763 episcopal visitation. National Library of Wales, Church in Wales LL/QA/1.)

A.14   Disdain the artifice they use
To bring in *Mass* and wooden shoes
With *Transubstantiation*.
Remember James the Second's reign
When glorious William broke the chain
Rome had put on this nation.
To abler heads leave state affairs
Give railing o'er, and say your prayers
For store of corn and hay.
With politics ne'er break your sleep
But ring your hogs, and worm your sheep
And rear your lambs and calves,
And royal George will take such care
That Rome and France no more shall dare
Attempt to make you slaves.

(Poem on the accession of George I (1714) found in the papers of Philip Williams of Dyffryn, Glamorgan. National Library of Wales, Penrice and Margam MS A142.)

A.15   Indeed, I never restrain him from going to prayers anywhere. I own I once advised him not to go to those in town as I had been informed it had been complained of to Mr Bullock by some ill-disposed people here, and might draw on a prosecution, as had been once attempted upon David Anthony for teaching a little school here, and the then Mayor and I were summoned before the Judges upon it, and Sergeant Skinner also sent for me and assured me he had Lord Chancellor's orders to examine and report the affair to him. The poor man was therefore obliged to desist and go to London to avoid trouble, such was the virulence of those times, and I don't think them a bit [. . . ?] here, but I solemnly protest I only advised without insisting on his not going even there, and as to my refusing his going elsewhere, he declares he never intended to say it, and thinks you have mistook him.

(Letter of Charles Halfpenny, Monmouth, to Jane Huddleston, 1754. Cambridgeshire Record Office, Huddleston MS JH84.)

A.16   At Colonel Holt's, an egg was found in a woodpile with several more in the hay next, that had on the top a spread eagle embossed as fit as the most ingenious arts could have done; on the shell, this motto:
Serve God with fear
Lewis's fall draws near.

(Notation on a Neath document *c.*1710. National Library of Wales, Penrice and Margam MS A102.)

A.17   Henllys, February the last, 1708/9
Reverend Sir,
You may very well conclude me carelessly negligent of my promise made to you when I was at Mount Radford, about transmitting you a full particular of the hard and villainous usage the clergy of Glamorgan received in the time of the usurpation and anarchy; but I protest I can justly plead not guilty, for *maugre* all the care and industry I used to come at a perfect account of all within this county both in the diocese of Llandaff and St Davids, early engaging my good friend the Reverend Mr Francis Davies, Prebend of Llandaff and nephew to the suffering Bishop of that name, he could not perfect it for me to send it till Thursday, last, nay though he had some time before by accident seen some accounts of the poor allowances paid by the understrapping sequestrators, at one of their widow's houses, yet when he came to her to desire her to see them again, she obstinately refused it, by which we guess that she was warned not to do it by some of the *Calamy* faction. I hope I am not yet too late to transmit what I have to you, which you may depend upon to be correctly authentic. Be pleased to advise me by the next post and I will carefully send it.
Edward Mansell

(Letter to John Walker, Bodleian Library (Oxford), MS Walker C4 fo.65.)

A.18   Glamorganshire 1715
Let the Commission of Peace for the County of Glamorgan be
renewed, and add thereto the persons following, placing all of
them of the *Quorum*:
The Hon. Jocelyn Sydney Esq.
Tho. Matthews of Llandaff, *armiger*
Philip Williams of Dyffryn, *armiger*
Charles Talbot, *armiger*
George Howell of Bovill, *armiger*
William Aubrey of Pencoed, *armiger*
Jeremiah Dawkins, *armiger*
George Howell of Roath, Barrister at Law
And you are likewise to leave out of the said commission:
Richard Savors, asm.
Iltid Nicholl, cler.
James Harris, cler.
William Lewis, cler.
To the Clerk of the Crown or his Deputy.
Fiat Commissio 10 die January 1714/5 (signed) Cowper.

(Public Record Office, C234/85.)

A.19   Thus Ended the year 1735, famous for nothing remarkable in
England, but for the daily depredations of the Spaniards upon
the English Merchants, and no redress to be hoped for — the
English Ministry being held in every Court in Europe in the
utmost contempt; and tho they have as great a Fleet now, as ever
England had, in time of War, besides a Standing Army
maintained these several years in time of peace to the Number of
above 20000 men, yet no use are made of all these to right the
Merchants, and retrive ye glory of Old England, but are made
use of at home to force obedience to cruell Tyrannicall Laws,
which otherwise would never be complyed with.

(Bulkeley diary, 1736, quoted in Evans, *Anglesey*, p.124.)

A.20   Cousin Pryse, Mr Pugh of Mathafarn, Will Powell, Mr William
Barlow and some other gentlemen of quality [met] at a

gentleman's house at Aberystwyth. They drank to [the *Pretender*'s] health and return upon their knees.

(Letter from John Meyricke of Bush (Pembs.) to Lord Mansell of Glamorgan, November 1710. National Library of Wales, Penrice and Margam MS L695.)

A.21 [Lord Mansell must] care what the world says of you, at least on this occasion, and consequently come to town, for indeed, my Lord, no-one knows how soon it may be his/own case, and I believe everyone would expect their friends' attendance when their lives and estates are at stake.

(Robert Mansell to his father, Lord Mansell, 12 March 1723. National Library of Wales, Penrice and Margam MS L1075.)

A.22 Today was ye first meeting of the *Jacobite* club at Llanerchymedd for this year, where all the noted *Tories* and *Jacobites* of this country have constantly met once a month these 2 years, and this year Mr Lewis of Llysdulas entered himself amongst them.

(Bulkeley diary, 1738, quoted in Evans, *Anglesey*, p.130.)

A.23 Ken ye wha comes here
Tis the Lord of all the clan
Whom we love so dear
Come ye bonny Highland lads
With your bonnets and your plaids
Come draw your trusty blades
And standard in the rear

(*Chorus*)
    Receive him as you can
    He's a bonny muckle man
    And nephew to Queen Anne
    Whom we loved so dear.

From Perth to Scoon
Intrepid he goes on
That's the course he'll steer
Like the Northern Star he'll light

Our wandering steps by night,
Never fail to set us right
Then banish fear.

(*Chorus*)

(1745 poem in National Library of Wales, Picton Castle MS
1492.)

A.24 . . . the town mob had for a long time with impunity maimed
several persons, beat out the brains of the barber at the Red
Lion . . . so that it was necessary to send for guards; and . . . a
strong party arrived from Pembrokeshire, who were quartered
at the Red Lion and elsewhere; upon this, the mob reinforced
themselves with men from the country and having fortified the
castle and upper-house, made port-holes, &c and supplied
themselves with great guns and small arms. The upper gate is
fortified by the Red Lion people and called Newgate, where the
prisoners taken by the *sheriffs* on one side are put . . . In short,
the town is full of fire, smoke and tumult . . . By an advertise-
ment published in the papers, the true cause of all this is the
violence of party, and a dislike to the *Jacobites*.

(*Gentleman's Magazine*, December 1755, p.570. Account of the
Carmarthen riots, November 1755: quoted by A.G. Prys-Jones
in *The Story of Carmarthenshire*, Swansea, 1972, Vol.II, p.309.)

A.25 Duke Beaufort, they say
Was forced to give way
And Sawney was lost in the wood
Dick Aubrey and Birt
Fell into the dirt
When Wyndham for liberty stood.

(*Chorus*)
    My brave boys
    when Wyndham for Liberty stood.

One like Arthur of old
Twas Talbot the bold
Attacked them in resolute mood

And Jones of Fonmon
Great liberty's son
With Wyndham for liberty stood.

(*Chorus*)

Gough, Aubrey, Treharne
Rees, Nicholl and Carne
With Llewellin of true British blood
Tredegar was there
And Gwinnett the Fair
With Wyndham for liberty stood.

(*Chorus*)

Landeg, Lucas and Rous
Valued lords not a sous
But lashed them with infamy's rod
Bassett joining the chase
Preferred death to disgrace
And with Wyndham for liberty stood.

(National Library of Wales, Tredegar MS 72/75.)

A.26 The man who lives happy, from cities remote
In his stockings of yarn and his brown russet coat
If he has but enough to live decent and neat
Is a fool if he cringe to the rich and the great.

(A.25 and A.26 are songs composed for the Wyndham campaign in Glamorganshire, 1789. National Library of Wales, Tredegar MS 72/83.)

A.27 Hang foxhounds and also those kinds of sad dogs called foxhunters who import foxes into the county for the savage sport of hunting them, of breaking their tenants' gates and fences and otherwise injure them. Fortunately for the world, they sometimes in breaking down a five barred gate break their own necks. Amen. So be it.

(Iolo Morganwg, *c.*1790. Quoted in G.J. Williams, *Iolo Morganwg*, Cardiff, 1956, Vol.I, p.26.)

A.28   I am sorry for your scarcity, but the complaint is almost general, we have indeed no dearth but an artificial scarcity of grain which bears a prodigious price from the collusion of the farmers and badgers. The colliers have rose in great numbers and plundered some barges, and the river is not quite open yet, but we have a company of soldiers, and I hope the Parliament will soon redress this grievance.

> (Letter of Charles Halfpenny, Monmouth, 1756. Cambridge-shire Record Office, Huddleston MS JH96.)

A.29   To the Honnered Magistrates & Elders of Swanze
This is the Generall Complaint of the Poor and Distressed.
First, That the farmers doth aske for the korn that we Can harly get Bread for our Starving familise.
Second; That the Millarts doth take a Quarter which is the fourth of a Peck for Towel.
Theredly; That the Molsters doth agree with the farmers for the Bearly Ho bring three bushel to the Market and open One and Caring the Rest to Theiar houses Instant for One John Vos and others and Likewise, the Bakers takeing in the Wheat In the Week Comming to Meet them in Mylls.
Now Sirs We hope that Wisdom will teach You that have Authority to order these Things.
Or Else we cannot Perrish without--Reveng we dwo intend two Meet together on the Borough of Crynlyn on the 29th Day of November 1766.
> God Save the King

> (Anonymous letter, quoted by E.P. Thompson in D. Hay *et al.*, *Albion's Fatal Tree*, London, 1977, p.327.)

A.30   Verses
Written on seeing a Man with a heavy Load on his Back and an Oak Leaf in his Hat on the 29th of May.

Poor fellow, what is it to you,
Or King, or *Restoration?*
'Twill make no difference to you,
Whoever rules the nation.

Still must thy back support the load,
Still bend thy back with toil;
Still must thou trudge the self-same road,
While great ones share the spoil.

(Poem by Sir Charles Hanbury Williams, in Gwyn Jones (Ed.),
Oxford Book of Welsh Verse in English, Oxford, 1977, p.117.)

Debating the Evidence

Philip Jenkins has chosen thirty extracts from contemporary documents, nearly half of them taken from private letters, several taken from
the remarkable diary of William Bulkeley, an Anglesey squire; no fewer
than six are poems. The selection is completed by a miscellany of sources
which defy classification. This variety of sources makes Dr Jenkins's
selection particularly lively reading; the letters and the diary extracts
provide notably intimate glimpses of the writers and their world.
Intimate yes, but can one necessarily trust in their being sincere, candid
and truthful?

Source A.1

Sir Arthur Owen of Orielton is alleged in this petition to have been
attempting to extend his control over the borough and *burgesses* of
Pembroke. Traditionally the *burgesses* of Tenby and Wiston (the latter a
thoroughly decayed borough) also had the right to vote in an election
for the member for Pembroke, and it is the mayor and *burgesses* of Wiston
that are here petitioning the House of Commons. Their rights were
upheld by the House in 1712 and Sir Arthur was unseated. How did
Owen attempt to secure his control over the election at Pembroke,
according to the allegations from Wiston?

Source A.2

Contested elections were avoided as far as possible (because of the
expense and disturbances which they were liable to cause) by agreements
between the gentry factions. Here the Duke of Bolton (owner, in the
right of his wife, of the Golden Grove estate in Carmarthenshire)
reproves Sir Nicholas Williams of Edwinsford for opposing Edward
Rice of Newtown (Dynevor). Rice received 593 votes, Williams 588, but
on petition to the House of Commons Williams was awarded the seat.

Mid-eighteenth-century wine glasses engraved with Jacobite insignia and mottoes. (*Source: National Museum of Wales.*)

What does this extract tell us of the power structure in eighteenth-century Carmarthenshire?

Source A.3
This letter lifts the veil which normally conceals deals of the kind described (or alleged), where a group of Monmouthshire *magnates* agreed to share out the two county seats ('*knights* of the shire') and the borough seat ('*burgess* of Monmouth'). The more powerful landlords took the county seats (which carried the greater prestige), leaving the borough seat to the less important man. (John Arnold never held the borough seat again).

Source A.4

At a by-election in Glamorgan following Lord Mansell's succession to the peerage, Thomas Matthews was the *Whig* candidate and Sir Charles Kemys-Tynte the *Tory*, the latter enjoying the support of three of the county's greatest *magnates*: Beaufort, Windsor and Mansell. The support of Charles Edwin of Llanmihangel was, however, crucial for the *Tories* and he drove a hard bargain. What, roughly, was that bargain? (Edwin was the sitting MP for Westminster; at the next general election in 1747 he was elected for Glamorgan).

Source A.5

This account of the uncontested election of Nicholas Bayly for Anglesey in 1734 comes from the diary of William Bulkeley, a minor squire but a kinsman of the dominant Lord Bulkeley who directed the political affairs of the island from his seat at Baron Hill, near Beaumaris. The election was a formality and it had doubtless been 'fixed' beforehand by the leading landowners. Even in an uncontested election the traditional dinner for the gentry and beer for the populace had to be given by the new MP.

Source A.6

William Bulkeley, the diarist, comments on the death of Sir Watkin Williams Wynn, the powerful *Tory* MP for Denbighshire. Note the cost of maintaining an 'interest'. What exactly does that term mean?

Source A.7

John Watkin of Cefn Brynich, near Brecon, writes to Lord Mansell to excuse himself for not voting for Mansell's preferred candidate in the Breconshire election of 1722. Comment on the dilemma in which a man having two landlords might find himself. (Watkin was probably a voter on the strength of holding a three-life lease of land worth more than forty shillings a year; he would be thus technically a *freeholder*, but would be very much dependent upon the favour of his landlord who had granted the lease.) Does this letter strike you as sincere?

Source A.8

What is the legal significance of this certificate signed by the rector of Llangelynnin?

Source A.9

The date of this letter must be 11 January 1712 (that is 'New Style' — 'Old Style' dates took the year as beginning on 25 March), since Sir Thomas Mansell was raised to the peerage on 1 January 1712 (New Style). Mansell was a member of the (*Tory*) Harley ministry and the reference to 'our late deliverance' may perhaps be to the defeat of the *Whigs* in the general election of 1710.

Source A.10

The *Tories* were in the ascendant both locally and nationally from 1710 until the death of Queen Anne in 1714. 'My Lord' is, of course, Lord Mansell; Sir Peter King, a leading *Whig* politician and later Lord Chancellor, had married into a Glamorgan family with important Swansea connections.

Source A.11

The clergy could still invoke the spectre of *Oliver Cromwell*'s time as late as 1790. It is interesting to note that Thomas Davies of Coity was a *Methodist* sympathizer.

Source A.12

This is a crude piece of anti-*Dissenter* verse. Summarize Henry Moore's view of the *Dissenters*.

Source A.13

The Bishop of Llandaff had asked each beneficed clergyman for information about (*inter alia*) the number of *Dissenters* in his parish. The rector of Merthyr Tydfil reports the sorry state of his parish overrun by all kinds of sects. But Merthyr was not a typical Welsh parish in 1763; it was another generation or more before most of Wales took on its nineteenth-century Nonconformist character.

Source A.14

It may be difficult for us to comprehend why eighteenth-century people were pathologically afraid of *Roman Catholicism*. The occasion of this poem is the succession of Protestant *George of Hanover* (rather than the *Catholic* James Stuart) on the death of Queen Anne in 1714. Think about the implications of what this anonymous poet says about the close connection between religion and politics at this date. Does this close connection explain why *Roman Catholicism* was so much feared?

Source A.15
What does this letter reveal of the discretion with which prominent *Catholics* practised their religion even as late as 1754?

Source A.16
This is a curious item referring to King *Louis XIV* of France, with whom Britain was at war in 1710. Is it perhaps merely a joke?

Source A.17
John Walker of Exeter was engaged in compiling his book on the 'sufferings' of the Anglican clergy during the *Civil War* and Common-wealth. It was published in 1714 with the title *An Attempt towards Recovering an Account of the Numbers and Sufferings of the Clergy*. His helpers in Glamorgan were Francis Davies of Llandaff and Edward Mansell of Henllys in Gower. Walker's work was the Anglican counterblast to *Edmund Calamy*'s book on the sufferings of Nonconformist ministers turned out of their livings in 1660–2, following the *Restoration* of Charles II. Why do you think such events of half a century before were still controversial in the reign of Queen Anne?

Source A.18
This is one of the few documents in this selection which mean exactly what they say — there is no room for interpretation, though some background information will help to bring out its political significance. Following the accession of *George I* and the return to power of the *Whigs*, the new Lord Chancellor (Lord Cowper) is adding his party's supporters to, and purging some of the opposition supporters from, the Com-mission of the Peace for Glamorgan — that is, the list of magistrates or *justices of the peace*.

Source A.19
What might be the value to historians of William Bulkeley's comments on the affairs of the country in the year 1735?

Sources A.20 and A.21
These two letters were written to Lord Mansell of Margam, the first by a Pembrokeshire squire telling him about a group of *Jacobite* supporters in mid-Wales, the second by his son urging him to come to London, where the *Jacobite* Bishop *Atterbury* was on trial in the House of Lords. Lord

Mansell was not himself a *Jacobite*, but his son is known to have had direct dealings with the *Pretender*'s court in France.

Source A.22
There were, on the evidence of William Bulkeley, 'noted *Tories* and *Jacobites*' among the squires of Anglesey. Note that he brackets '*Tories* and *Jacobites*' together. Is this to some extent the partisan view of a *Whig*, or was there more than a taint of *Jacobitism* (that is, a lingering loyalty to the exiled Stuart dynasty) in the *Tory* party?

Source A.24
Party faction was strong in the town of Carmarthen and rioting broke out there in November 1755 between the town mob and the '*Jacobites*' whose headquarters were at the Red Lion. The report in the *Gentleman's Magazine* concludes with the comment that 'the true cause of all this is the violence of party, and a dislike to the *Jacobites*'. On the basis of a reading of Sources A.20–A.24 and Philip Jenkins's comments, assess the strength and nature of Welsh *Jacobitism*. To what extent do the documents reflect the biased views of party supporters?

Sources A.25 and A.26
These two poems were written in praise of Thomas Wyndham of Dunraven, the successful candidate in the Glamorgan election of 1789. The first mentions several Glamorgan gentry (some major, some minor) who were his supporters — and the supporters of 'liberty'. This was not a revolutionary sentiment, but rather a cry for the political independence of the gentry and *freeholders* from the influence of the absentee *Tory magnates*, such as the Duke of Beaufort, Lord Mountstuart (the future Marquess of Bute) and Lord Vernon. The second poem pictures the popular contemporary stereotype of the 'yeoman', a figure much regarded as the backbone of his country. Perhaps the reality was somewhat different.

Source A.27
Iolo Morganwg (or *Edward Williams*, stonemason) — as will be further seen in Gwyn A.Williams's chapter — was a democrat and a radical, one who welcomed the *French Revolution* in 1789. In his private letters and unpublished writings he has many savage things to say about the Glamorgan gentry, particularly those who neglected their duty to the

Richard Jones Gwynne of Taliaris, Sea Serjeant. (*Source: National Museum of Wales.*)

community for the pursuit of pleasure. In this extract does he hint at a growing class conflict between landlords and farmers?

Source A.28
During food shortages in the eighteenth century there was always someone who laid the blame on farmers and dealers ('badgers' were corn-dealers) for creating artificial scarcities for their own profit. There may have been something in this explanation, but a bad harvest was usually the fundamental cause. (The colliers referred to are those of the Forest of Dean; the river is the Wye which was navigable by barge as far up as Monmouth).

Source A.29
The authentic voice of the poor is rarely heard. Here the poor and distressed of Swansea have dared to address — and to threaten — the local magistrates in November 1766. The demand, as in so many of these incidents in the eighteenth century, was for food to be sold at a reasonable price. Despite the threatening tone of the letter, note the concluding expression of loyalty to the Crown — these were no revolutionaries. What exactly is the main complaint of the poor in the paragraph beginning 'Theredly'? (millarts = millers; towel = toll (?); ho = who; molsters = maltsters; bearly = barley; caring = carrying; borough of Crynlyn = Crymlyn Burrows.)

Source A.30
Sir Charles Hanbury Williams, a considerable landowner in Mon-mouthshire and a sophisticated littérateur, politician and diplomat, was well known for his satirical verse and political lampoons written from a *Whig* standpoint. What was the significance of the oak leaf worn on 29 May, and how does this particular satire reflect the writer's politics?

Discussion

Diaries and letters present particular problems to the historian. To a greater or lesser extent they are autobiographical; they provide insight into the thoughts, attitudes and lives of their writers in a way that no other sources at this distance of time can do. They are the most intimate and revealing of documents — and in this lies their undeniable value as historical evidence — but what exactly they reveal either about the writer himself or herself or about his or her external world will rarely be easy to determine. In order to interpret each piece of writing we would ideally need to know about, for example, the circumstances of the writer, his position in society, his education, his political and religious affiliations, his temperament and his character.

It may well be that William Bulkeley, the squire of Llanfechell, (Sources A.5, A.6, A.19, A.22) was keeping a diary purely for his own satisfaction and that he expected no one to read what he had written. If this is so, he was committing to paper his private thoughts and personal record of events without the need to dissemble or to consider how anyone would react. He thus wrote the 'truth' as it seemed to him. With a quarter of a century's constant diary writing available to us (1734–43 and 1747–60: the volume for 1743–7 is missing), it becomes possible to come to some degree of understanding of the man, his motives and opinions, as well as the external circumstances of his life or his place in Anglesey society, and thus to achieve some success in interpreting the daily autobiography which he has bequeathed to posterity.

Letters are even more difficult to assess, except when a particular writer's letters have survived in quantity. The character and social status of the letter-writer are again crucial, but so are his relationship to the recipient of the letter and his purpose in writing. What he writes to one person may be different in ways both obvious and subtle from what he writes to another. Thus the way a man would write to his landlord (for example, Source A.7) would need quite a different assessment from what a man might write to his father (for example, Source A.21); what a man wrote to his father might depend very much upon the degree of intimacy which existed between them. The problem, of course, is that it may not be possible to find out all the background information which would be needed to illuminate all the relevant factors. These remarks apply equally to letters included among the sources in other chapters of this book.

Poems are different from diaries and letters, though the poems quoted here (Sources A.12, A.14, A.23, A.25, A.26) are political rather than literary and they scarcely deserve the attention of a literary critic. The poems are used as vehicles for strong partisan or propagandist statements, for example in support of election candidates (Sources A.25, A.26). They are sources for contemporary political ideas, but they should obviously be treated with some considerable reserve.

The Calvinistic Methodist Fathers. (*Source: National Library of Wales.*)

The New Enthusiasts

GERAINT H. JENKINS

One of the most powerful influences in the remaking of Wales in the eighteenth century was enthusiasm. Those who counted themselves enthusiasts were characterized by the consciousness of a New Birth, infectious zeal, warm personal piety, pulpit eloquence, and a general distrust of rationalism and radical politics. Most of these people were committed to the *Methodist* cause and were prepared to propagate their views with unusual vigour. In its initial stages, *Methodism* was a fluid, amorphous movement whose excessive zeal and stress on the emotions were not to everyone's taste. In the longer term, however, it became a triumphantly successful religion and it played a notable part in the creation of Nonconformist Wales. There is no doubt that it brought enormous spiritual joy and satisfaction to thousands of Welsh people. Led by eye-catching young preachers and exhorters who believed that the world was their parish, the *Methodist* movement created an army of enthusiasts. Its emphasis on soul-searching preaching, intimate fellowship and fervent hymn-singing made *Methodism* an attractive religion, especially among pious and relatively well-to-do farmers and craftsmen in rural communities. It taught its members to identify religion with the regeneration of the soul and it planted within them certain moral values and devotional habits which became an intrinsic part of their daily lives. As *Methodism* grew, the new enthusiasts injected new life into the religion of friends, rivals and even potential enemies. Their emphasis on zeal, piety, commitment and strict morality left its mark on many Anglican clergymen. Their enthusiasm also helped to sustain the remarkably successful Welsh *circulating schools* which, by providing common people with easy access to elementary schooling, enabled peasants and their children to acquire the basic skills of literacy. Moreover, the preoccupation of *Methodists* with salvation persuaded many *Dissenting* groups to recover the sense of mission which had been such a notable feature of the labours of their *Puritan* forebears in the seventeenth century. After 1760 in particular, Welsh *Dissent* caught the revivalist enthusiasm and in the process became a more popular evangelical movement. As the decades rolled by, groups over a wide spectrum of religious experience resolved to carry out energetic missionary activity in order to win souls to Christ. Over the century as a whole, therefore, the new enthusiasts helped to generate, satisfy and sustain the growing demand for piety, morality, education and self-improvement.

A substantial and valuable corpus of diaries, letters, sermons, elegies, epics, hymns and prose works was produced by enthusiasts in the eighteenth century. For instance, Howel Harris, the imperious founder of the *Methodist* movement, has left 296 volumes of diaries (covering the years 1735–73) as well as thousands of letters. Harris was an insatiable letter-writer. Much to the distress of his correspondents (as well as future historians), however, his letters were written in a tiny, closely-written and barely decipherable hand. Some of his colleagues were just as prolific. William Williams, Pantycelyn, the supreme literary artist of the day and the greatest of Welsh hymn-writers, composed 860 hymns and a series of remarkable prose works. But although this material provides a vivid portrait of the hopes, fears and achievements of Welsh enthusiasts, it must be treated with care. Many *Methodist* chroniclers, carried away by their own enthusiasm, wrote dramatic accounts which strain our credulity.

It was, nonetheless, natural for *Methodists* to sing the praises of their own movement and to detect the hand of God on their labours. They fervently believed that the trumpet voice of their evangelists had awakened a slumbering people. Williams Pantycelyn, the movement's most celebrated mouthpiece and historian, declared that pre-*Methodist* Wales was a valley of dry bones (B.1). Gripped by spiritual lethargy and moral decadence, its people stood in urgent need of regeneration. By skilfully

B.1

using striking images such as 'light' and 'heat', Pantycelyn was able to portray *Methodism* as a movement which brought new passion and energy into the national life of Wales. The momentous turning-point, he argued, came in 1735 when Howel Harris of Trefeca and Daniel Rowland of Llangeitho experienced sensational conversions. Bound together by their common experience of the New Birth and their desire to save souls, these young men dedicated their lives to deepening the spiritual lives of their fellow countrymen. Of late, however, historians have re-examined this view and the pendulum has swung perceptibly against the notion that Wales experienced a 'Great Awakening' in 1735.

In many ways, the seeds of *Methodism* had not only already been sown but were beginning to grow vigorously. From the *Restoration* period onwards, Anglican clergymen and *Dissenting* ministers had been exercising a much more effective pastoral oversight over their flocks than ever before. Sermons were being preached more regularly. The number of religious books in Welsh had increased dramatically in the wake of the development of provincial printing presses. 'Middling sorts' had acquired the reading habit and literacy rates were rising. These genuine improvements meant that Welsh people, especially farmers, craftsmen and artisans, were capable of responding favourably to the *Methodist* message. There was B.2 clearly a widespread thirst for religion (B.2), and in unguarded moments even the new enthusiasts confessed (in private) that Wales offered fertile soil for men with a mission. In his diary, *John Wesley* admitted he was fortunate in finding the times B.3 highly propitious (B.3). By the 1730s Wales was 'ripe for the Gospel'.

It would be rash, too, to endorse the dewy-eyed *'Methodist'* view that the power of the Holy Spirit transformed religious life over the whole of Wales in the eighteenth century. Nineteenth-century historians, in particular, were convinced that *Methodism* had set Wales ablaze. More recent scholars, however, are in the main agreed that the growth of *Methodism* was a slow, uneven and fitful process. Howel Harris and his colleagues scored their greatest successes in south Wales, notably in the areas surrounding their principal headquarters at Llanddowror,

The Welch Curate. (Source: British Museum.)

Llangeitho and Trefeca. In north Wales the strength of the Established Church and widespread hostility to enthusiasm barred the way to dramatic success. Elsewhere, too, personal animosities, theological differences and sectional interests were formidable obstacles facing young evangelists. Yet they were more than able to take advantage of the obvious flaws within the structure of the Established Church in the penurious dioceses of St Davids and Llandaff. As *Evan Evans* (Ieuan Brydydd Hir) trenchantly pointed out, 'the hand of sacrilege

B.4   [had] pressed sore on this country at the *Reformation*' (B.4). The Church had been robbed of its wealth by lay impropriators. This had led to a wide disparity between the wealth and comforts of the upper and lower clergy. In many parts of the large, rambling and impoverished diocese of St Davids, curates were so badly paid that they found it virtually impossible to carry out their pastoral responsibilities effectively. 'As ragged as a Welsh curate' was a popular saying in the eighteenth century, and many contemporary cartoons poked fun at the rustic, skinny and unkempt Welsh clergy. It is not surprising, therefore, that *Methodism* gained most ground in those communities in south Wales where clergymen, for a variety of reasons, neglected their flocks. Low standards of pastoral care and infrequent preaching persuaded many disaffected church-goers, and even *Dissenters*, to turn to *Methodism* for spiritual comfort and guidance.

The *Methodist* movement also capitalized on its Welshness. As the decades rolled by, the Established Church lost its traditional image as *y fam eglwys* (the mother church) and the long-term trend was towards *Dissent*. Part of the problem lay in the remarkably obtuse policy of successive governments of appointing English, Scottish or Irish bishops to sees in Wales. Between 1727 and 1870 not a single Welsh-speaking bishop was appointed to serve in Wales. In many ways, this short-sighted policy helped to rob the Established Church of its vitality. Both religious reformers and cultural patriots censured the *Esgyb Eingl* (English bishops) who made no effort to conceal their contempt for the Welsh language and who laid plans to drive

B.5   the Welsh Bible and Prayer Book out of Welsh churches (B.5). Critics like *Evan Evans, Lewis Morris* and *William Jones,* Llangadfan, constantly bemoaned the appointment of idle,

The Welch Parson. (*Source: British Museum.*)

absentee prelates who spoke no Welsh and seldom visited Wales. Their neglect, it was argued, brought the Church into disrepute. It also encouraged the appointment of English clergymen to the most favoured livings in Wales, a practice which incensed talented Welsh candidates who failed to climb the ladder of preferment. The celebrated *Morris Letters* of the mid-eighteenth century are riddled with angry letters from embittered rural clerics who were powerless to prevent their parishioners from joining the *Methodist* cause (B.6).

B.6

But Welsh *Methodism* was not simply the product of abuses and shortcomings within the administrative structure of the Established Church. It was, by its very nature, a positive, outward-going and dynamic force. *Methodist* preachers were men of boundless zeal and enthusiasm. Their bulky journals and copious letters give the impression of men akin to Ben Jonson's Zeal-of-the-land-Busy. Although keenly aware that they were setting out on new and probably perilous paths, they were determined to win souls. Convinced that they had received a commission from Christ, they resolved to bring Satan's kingdom tumbling down. The new enthusiasts travelled widely in order to bring the Gospel to miserable sinners. Like their *Puritan* forebears, but on a much wider scale, they preached in the open air as well as in churches. Powerful sermons were delivered in churchyards, fields, fairs, markets, barns and stables. Howel Harris, the principal standard-bearer of the *Methodist* cause in Wales, was a man of superhuman energy. His journal conveys most vividly the trials and tribulations which beset the tireless evangelist. Harris drove himself to the point of exhaustion in his efforts to win souls and reform lives (B.7). He travelled from village to village and from town to town, usually on horseback (with a slack rein in order to enable him to read during his journey). Often he preached six or seven times each day during his tours. Although troubled from time to time by toothache, piles and gout, Harris contented himself with a few hours' sleep at night. Little wonder that his body often ached so much that he could scarcely move. But his staying-power and resolution were remarkable. Such was his concern for the salvation of sinners he was willing to travel in fair and foul weather to all corners of the land. Many of those who witnessed

B.7

his powerful sermons believed that here, indeed, was a very
B.8   special person (B.8).

Methodism was novel and exciting, and its preachers drew
large and expectant crowds wherever they went. Their sermons
were often filled with fierce attacks on the evils of drunkenness,
idleness, lust and debauchery. Their horrendous descriptions of
hell sent shivers of apprehension through their listeners.
Congregations were constantly reminded of the awfulness of sin
and the urgent need for repentance and salvation. Many
sermons were so impassioned that those hearers who experienced the pangs of the New Birth indulged in wild, convulsive
physical movements. In their letters and diaries, *Methodist*
leaders often experienced great difficulty in conveying the
B.9   essence of these manifestations (B.9). No one was more capable
of inducing paroxysms among members of his congregation
than Daniel Rowland, the silver-voiced preacher who made the
tiny village of Llangeitho the principal Mecca of Welsh
Methodism. When this 'second Paul' delivered his mesmerizing
sermons, cries of 'what must I do to be saved?' echoed around
the church and churchyard. Members of Rowland's congregation often roared, trembled, wept, sang, clapped their hands, or
fell to their knees on the ground. Uncommitted onlookers, who
looked upon this kind of hysteria-raising with a disapproving,
even cynical eye, believed that 'greater instances of madness'
B.10   were seldom seen even in *Bedlam* (B.10). Daniel Rowland's
melodic voice, theatrical gestures and emotional message
produced powerful mental and physical stresses among his
hearers which found release in quaking, leaping, dancing and
singing. His flocks were dubbed 'the Welsh Jumpers' by
derisive English satirists. Others called them 'the Holy Rollers'.
Not everyone, however, shared Rowland's taste for public
demonstrations of praise. Staid churchmen, rational *Dissenters*
and enemies of enthusiasm loudly condemned spiritual gym-
nastics of this kind. Many of those who sobbed, cried out,
fainted, and gnashed their teeth, it was argued, were terrified by
fears of the torment of hell and the prospect of eternal
damnation. *Methodist* preachers never shrank from what they
considered to be their duty to remind sinners of the horrors of
B.11   the unquenchable fire in hell (B.11). Given these circumstances,

it is not surprising that 'the Welsh Jumpers' were accused of
lunacy, hysteria and diabolical possession. The first epigraph on
the title-page of *Theophilus Evans*'s splenetic *The History of
Modern Enthusiasm* (1752) reads:

> Beware what spirit rages in your Breast
> For Ten inspir'd, Ten Thousand are possess'd.

Methodism offered other ways, too, for people to express their
spiritual experiences and emotional troubles. From 1737 onwards a network of closely-knit religious bands or societies was
established at grass-roots level. These tiny cells later came under
the watchful supervision of the central administrative body, the
Association (*Sasiwn*), the first of which was held at Defynnog in
Breconshire in 1742. By 1750, 428 *Methodist* societies had been
set up, mostly in the six counties of south Wales. The *seiat*
(society) was, in essence, a clinic for the soul, and a variety of
sources relating to society meetings throw well-focused light on
the nature of *Methodism*. The prose and hymns of William
Williams, Pantycelyn, who was himself an extremely well-
informed and perceptive exhorter and steward, enable us to
witness the inner spiritual struggles which enlivened or
bedevilled the lives of *Methodist* members in rural Wales.
Members assembled at night for two or three hours twice a
week to read the Scriptures, master the *catechism*, and above all,
tell of their joyous or troubled experiences. As they gathered
together in private houses or barns, they found genuine human
friendships and warm Christian fellowship. Even the most shy
and withdrawn in their midst were happy to avail themselves of
the opportunity to share their spiritual and emotional problems
with others. Sometimes, perhaps, the relentless soul-searching
embarked upon within the four walls of a society meeting
precipitated psychological stresses and feelings of inadequacy,
guilt and confusion. But stewards and counsellors were
generally hand-picked men, blessed with great patience and
wisdom. As Pantycelyn shows, the best of them were able to
persuade class-members to unburden themselves of their
B.12   problems and help them in their struggle against sin (B.12).
Particularly close and vigilant supervision was exercised over
young and unmarried males and females as they exchanged
spiritual and pre-marital experiences behind closed doors. Only

pious, devout and unspotted people gained admittance to such meetings. Those who failed to meet the exacting standards insisted upon by *Methodist* leaders were swiftly turned away; and unrepentant backsliders were summarily excommunicated from the fold.

The growth of *Methodism* also coincided with, and was dependent, to a greater or lesser degree, on the development of Griffith Jones's remarkably successful *circulating schools*. Like many of his fellow enthusiasts, Griffith Jones, rector of Llanddowror, genuinely believed that he had been singled out by God to save the souls of his fellow countrymen. His 'heavenly call' was a dramatic turning-point in his life; in its wake he became obsessed with the need to bring sinful peasants to repentance. Long before the youthful *Methodist* evangelists began to roam the length and breadth of Wales, Griffith Jones had acquired a reputation as a powerful and often fiery preacher. His enemies dubbed him 'a busy enthusiast', and his zeal, preaching style and selfless commitment to the cause of Protestantism left their mark on many young *Methodists* in the diocese of St Davids. Several *Methodist* leaders, notably Harris and Rowland, regarded Griffith Jones as their mentor and father confessor, and there is a lot to be said for the view that Llanddowror counts as much in the story of early *Methodism* as do Trefeca and Llangeitho. For a variety of reasons, however, Jones was forced to distance himself from his young *Methodist* colleagues because their irregular, and sometimes insolent, behaviour threatened to wreck his educational scheme. In order to gratify patrons of the *circulating schools*, Jones went so far as to condemn their 'rude enthusiasm', even though he himself had transgressed the rules and regulations of the Church during his youth.

Unlike his *Methodist* protégés, Griffith Jones believed that the provision of elementary schooling and the supply of cheap reading matter were required in order to enable peasants to understand fully the basic principles of the Christian faith. He was convinced that religious reformers had a duty to preach and teach Christian knowledge in a manner intelligible to the lower orders of society — those whom he often referred to as 'the vulgar sorts'. Aided, perhaps, by hypochondria and insomnia,

Griffith Jones became a remarkably energetic schools adminis-
trator and author. He was a dogged, persevering man who was
determined to provide poor people with the opportunity to
acquire at least the basic skills of literacy. Existing charity
schools, established and governed by the Society for the
Promotion of Christian Knowledge (SPCK), had failed to
achieve revolutionary results in Wales, partly because they were
geared to urban rather than rural needs, but mainly because of
the antipathy of its sponsors towards the Welsh language. Some
B.13   of Griffith Jones's contemporaries (B.13) had drawn attention
to the lifeless and unimaginative teaching by rote which
characterized English-medium schools in Wales, but Jones was
the first to establish a national network of schools in which the
overwhelming majority of pupils were taught through the
medium of Welsh.

When Griffith Jones launched his pioneering educational
scheme, based on itinerant schooling and a heavy emphasis on
Bible-reading and catechizing, his principal concern was to
adapt his sytem to peasant needs and interests. His annual
reports, *Welch Piety*, are a mine of information. In them we find,
from time to time, a number of persuasive letters which preach
the merits of the Welsh language. Cynical or parsimonious
patrons were shown how Jones's army of schoolmasters
capitalized on the phonetic nature of the Welsh orthography.
Under his scheme, Welsh children were no longer obliged to
grapple with material in a foreign tongue. As a result, they
learnt their letters swiftly, mastered lengthy portions of the
Scriptures, and became capable of giving a decent account of
their faith. Like all enthusiasts, Griffith Jones was acutely aware
that speed was essential; the follies of his predecessors had
meant that many hundreds of innocent and ignorant souls had
B.14   fallen into 'the dreadful Abyss of Eternity' (B.14). Fortified by
the selfless financial support of enthusiastic philanthropists like
Sir John Philipps of Picton Castle and Madam *Bridget Bevan* of
Laugharne, Jones was able to recruit talented schoolmasters,
distribute pious literature, and win the co-operation of local
clergymen. His scheme was flexible, economical and efficient.
Since the schools went directly to the poor, pupils — both
B.15   young and old (B.15) — were prepared to make considerable

sacrifices in order to master their letters and learn the basic Christian principles. Large numbers of tenants, labourers and servants were given their first opportunity to learn to read. Throughout Wales by the 1760s parish churches and farmsteads echoed to the sounds of adult and infant voices chanting the alphabet aloud, spelling words, repeating the *catechism*, and reading passages from the Bible or popular devotional books. Classes of between thirty and forty pupils were the norm, although in rural Carmarthenshire numbers were often much

B.16   higher, notably within night-schools (B.16). Farmsteads which housed these schools often served as *Methodist* seminaries, and it is evident that the cause of revivalism prospered as more and more people learnt to read. Welsh *Methodism* would never have borne so splendid a harvest in the eighteenth century had not Griffith Jones and his lieutenants sown such valuable seeds. Similarly, Church life was revitalized: parishioners worshipped more regularly and devoutly; monthly communion became the norm; and family prayers and devotional exercises were conducted on the hearth, in the workshop, and even in knitting groups. Hundreds of letters sent to Llanddowror by appreciative clergymen and gentlemen testified warmly to the bene-

B.17   ficial effects of regular schooling (B.17). Neighbouring parishes vied with each other for schoolmasters and sought to emulate each other's number of pupils. By the time of Griffith Jones's death in 1761, around a quarter of a million adults and children had learnt to read in Welsh *circulating schools*. This is, without doubt, one of the most remarkable success stories in the history of popular education in eighteenth-century Europe. Even Catherine the Great of Russia was deeply impressed when she received glowing accounts of the remarkable achievements of Griffith Jones and his itinerant schools.

In spite of these successes, it is important not to claim too much. Only a minority of the people of Wales heeded the trumpet blasts of the new enthusiasts. *Methodist* activity produced a torrent of critical and often abusive literature. Although this material — prepared by hostile witnesses — must be used with caution, it suggests that many people in Wales detested unbridled zeal and enthusiasm. In many quarters, *Methodist* successes were greeted with undisguised dismay. In

Lewis Morris. (*Source: National Museum of Wales.*)

the eyes of magistrates and clergymen, *Methodism* was a challenge to the establishment: *justices of the peace*, mindful of the bitter experiences of their forebears in the mid-seventeenth century, lived in fear of a new 'rule of the saints'. Among the clergy, too, enthusiasm aroused genuine suspicion; it was natural for them to become incensed whenever itinerant preachers humiliated them by calling them 'carnal priests', 'blind guides' and 'dumb dogs' in the presence of their

B.18   parishioners (B.18). The self-righteous and holier-than-thou attitude of re-born evangelists roused them to fury. Some clergymen, unable to suppress their anger, hired local mobs to heckle, stone and pelt *Methodist* preachers with rotten fruit. It was not uncommon, therefore, to see *Methodist* evangelists trudging wearily homewards, nursing bloody noses and bruised bodies.

Other enemies of the new enthusiasts adopted more subtle strategems. *Lewis Morris* (Llywelyn Ddu o Fôn), a prominent cultural patriot and a gifted satirist, was an arch-critic of all *Methodists. Morris* was not averse to scandal-mongering and mischief, and he produced a mock sermon which displayed a lively horror of everything which enthusiasts stood for. He offered the view that *Methodist* leaders not only preyed on innocent, credulous young women but also positively encouraged carnal lusts. These handsome and dynamic youths, he argued, lured young wenches to darkened houses where lewd

B.19   immoral acts were committed (B.19). It need hardly be said that such claims were grossly exaggerated, but at least they indicated how enthusiasts were prone to find themselves torn between spiritual and sexual lusts.

The fervent heat which *Methodism* generated was also anathema to small but highly vocal groups of rational *Dissenters* in Wales. Pugnacious *Arminian* and *Arian* ministers who laboured in what *Methodist* evangelists called 'Y Smotyn Du' (The Black Spot) in south Cardiganshire were appalled by the excessive enthusiasm displayed by Daniel Rowland's 'Jumpers'

B.20   in Llangeitho (B.20) and their blind faith in the power of the Holy Spirit. No people more tenaciously resisted the 'vital religion' of the revivalists than these hard-headed intellectuals. They believed that all *Methodists* dwelt in the realm of

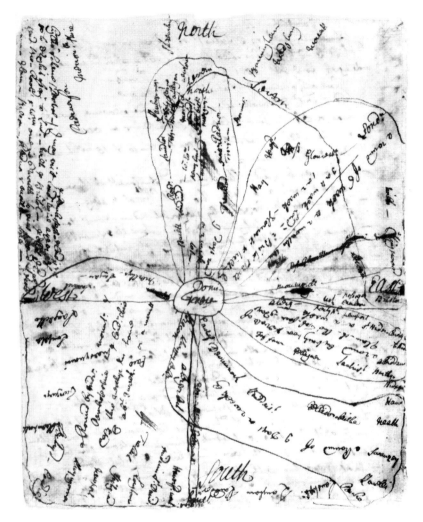

Howel Harris's map of his travels. (*Source: National Library of Wales and the Historical Society of the Presbyterian Church of Wales.*)

Cloud-cuckoo-land. In their eyes, enthusiasts were quietist, other-worldly, 'peculiar' people who set themselves apart from the rest of society. By slavishly preaching the duty of political obedience to their flocks, they offered few opportunities for impoverished people to right wrongs or to aspire above their station. Moreover, there was at least an element of truth in the claim that, by the end of the eighteenth century, *Methodism* had succeeded in spreading 'an universal gloom over the country'

B.21 (B.21). Not all Welsh people, by any means, were at ease in the company of *Methodists*. Nevertheless, the new enthusiasts had helped to remake Wales by encouraging pious middling sorts to set new standards of personal conduct and social morality. By the nineteenth century their values had become part and parcel of the way of life of thousands of Welsh people.

Sources

B.1   Spiritual death, love of the world, arid disputations, self-regard . . . night, night in all the churches . . . Ministers without talent, with no experience of grace, without simplicity, without a contrite heart, without faith . . . crawling like tail-wriggling serpents into houses, that is to say churches, for gain, profit or bodily sustenance, feeding on the fleece of the flock, with no care of souls . . . But now the day has dawned, the Lord has breathed upon the dry bones, and they are moving.

(William Williams, *Atteb Philo-Evangelius i Martha Philopur*, Carmarthen, 1763, in *Gweithiau William Williams, Pantycelyn*, Vol.II, ed. Garfield H. Hughes, Cardiff, 1967, pp.15–16.)

B.2   There is, I believe, no part of the Nation more inclin'd to be Religious, and to be delighted with it than the poor Inhabitants of these Mountains. They don't think it too much when neither ways, nor Weather are inviting, over cold and bleak Hills to travel three or four Miles, or more, on foot to attend the Publick Prayers, and sometimes as many more to hear a Sermon, and they seldom grudge many times for several Hours together in their damp and cold Churches, to wait the coming of their Minister, who by Occasional Duties in his other Curacy's, or by other Accidents may be oblig'd to disappoint them, and to be often variable in his Hours of Prayer.

(Erasmus Saunders, *A View of the State of Religion in the Diocese of St David's*, London, 1721, reprinted ed., Cardiff, 1949, p.32.)

B.3 I have seen no part of England so pleasant for sixty or seventy miles together as those parts of Wales I have been in. And most of the inhabitants are indeed ripe for the gospel. I mean (if the expression appear strange) they are earnestly desirous of being instructed in it.

(John Wesley's *Journal*, 20 October 1739, in *John Wesley in Wales 1739–1790*, ed. A.H. Williams, Cardiff, 1971, p.5.)

B.4 For the Inhabitants are a lot of such wild enthusiasts, and have such antipathy to a Clergyman as the most bigotted *Presbyterian* or Quaker. And after all their whine and cant are I believe in my conscience the most arrant rogues under the sun; an instance of which was their endeavour to deprive the poor old clergymen who served their church for upwards of three score years of his benefice, which persons of common humanity would hardly do to an old horse that had in his time been of service to them. The hand of sacrilege pressed sore on this country at the *reformation*, so that the little pittance that was left them in money sunk in value almost near to that of a hired servant in our days. This has produced that Hydra of sectaries with which it now abounds which are the spawn of the Fanatics in the times of Oliver's usurpation, when *Vavasor Powell* and other hot-headed enthusiasts at that time commenced Itinerant Preachers to replant the Gospel, but found no success in North Wales, there being a decent reputable set of clergy with good salaries; but here the clergy were such ignorant wretches, and because they were poor, made such a despicable appearance in the eyes of the vulgar, that they very soon quitted the Established Church, and are never like to return to it, as long as affairs stand in the condition they are now in.

(Evan Evans, curate of Lledrod, Llanwnnws and Capel Ieuan, to Richard Morris in London, 12 March 1767, in *Additional*

Letters of the Morrises of Anglesey (1735–1786), Part 2, ed. Hugh
Owen, London, 1949, pp.688–9.)

B.5   Wales is a conquered country, it is proper to introduce the
English language, and it is the duty of the bishops to endeavour
to promote the English, in order to introduce the language . . .
It has always been the policy of the legislature to introduce the
English language into Wales.

(The advocate for Dr Thomas Bowles, Court of Arches, 1773,
*The Depositions, Arguments and Judgement in the Cause of the Church-
Wardens of Trefdraeth against Bowles*, London, 1773.)

B.6   The consequence of having Englishmen Bishops will be, that
the people will either fall back to ignorance and superstition, or
be tost about by every blast of Enthusiasm, of which we have
too many pregnant and recent Instances already . . . The common Trades of Weavers, Smiths, Shoemakers, Taylors and the
very meanest handycrafts have furnished them with preachers
in abundance. And their followers afford them a larger salary
than what many a studious laborious Clergyman receives from
three churches that are impropriations.

(Evan Evans, 'The Grievances of the Principality of Wales in
the Church', c.1764. National Library of Wales MS 2009B,
pp.95–8.)

B.7   10 May, 1742. Bwlchgwynt, Meidrim. Exhorting sweet.
Toward Llanwinio. Discoursed sweet and clear. Toward
Pencnwc. The 3rd or 4th mile today. I heard that I am to be
taken here by a gent, that a warrant is sent for. Rejoiced for the
honour of suffering for Christ. NB I have not felt this long ago,
thought of going to prison sweet beyond expression, especially
of going to Carmarthen. Thought I would preach there to the
town, and that this was a means of sending me there, and so
came full of power. There met Bro.Howell Davies glorying in
the Cross now, which my flesh never could do. Discoursed to 7,
opposers did not come. Had amazing power to cut and tear.
Incited them to learn to read Welsh. With Bro.Howell Davies to
past 8. In praying in parting there came great power to unite my

soul to his in spirit. Near 9 towards St Kennox in Pembrokeshire, there near 1. Travelling today about 15 miles. Bed near 3.

(Howel Harris's *Journal*, 10 May 1742, in *Howel Harris's Visits to
Pembrokeshire*, ed. Tom Beynon, Aberystwyth, 1966.)

B.8 O what a flame was kindled! Never man spake, in my hearing, as
this man spake. What a nursing-father has God sent us! He has
indeed learned of the good Shepherd to carry the lambs in his
bosom. Such love, such power, such simplicity was irresistible.
The lambs dropped down on all sides into their shepherd's
arms. Those words broke out like thunder, 'I now find a
commission from God to invite all poor sinners, justified or
unjustified, to His altar; and I would not for ten thousand
worlds be the man that should keep any from it. There I first
found Him myself. That is the place of meeting.'

(Charles Wesley's *Journal*, ed. Thomas Jackson, London, 1849,
Vol. 1, pp. 226–7.)

B.9 The Manner of the Itinerant's holding-forth is generally very
boisterous and shocking, and adapted, to the best of their skill,
to alarm the Imagination, and to raise a Ferment in the Passions,
often attended with screaming and trembling of the Body. The
Preacher now grows more tempestuous and dreadful in his
Manner of Address, stamps and shrieks, and endeavours all he
can to increase the rising Consternation, and is sometimes
spread over a great Part of the Assembly in a few Minutes from
its first Appearance. And, to compleat the Work, the Preacher
has Recourse still to more frightful Representations; that he sees
Hell-Flames flashing in their Faces; and they are now! now!
now! dropping into Hell! into the Bottom of Hell! the Bottom
of Hell!.

(Theophilus Evans, *The History of Modern Enthusiasm*, London,
1752, National Library of Wales, Trefeca Letters, no. 745.)

B.10 This Day I heard Dear Bro. Rowlands, and such a sight mine
Eyes never saw. I can send you no true Idea thereof. Such Light
and Power there was in the Congregation as can't be expressed.

By Hundreds ye People went from one parish Church to another, 3 Miles away, singing and rejoicing in God, and so having communicated of ye Lord's Supper together, came so many Miles again to Night . . .

(Howel Harris to George Whitefield, 5 October 1742, in *Cylchgrawn Cymdeithas Hanes y Methodistiaid Calfinaidd*, Vol. 1, no. 2, 1916, p. 54.)

B. 11 As I happened once to lodge of a Saturday night within ¼ mile of Mr Daniel Rowland, a *Methodistical* clergyman and a relation of mine, I went to his church ye Sunday following where I own I heard a pretty good discourse (as far as I could hear) delivered to a very large congregation. While he was performing Divine Service, the people seemed to behave quietly and somewhat devoutly, but as they began to sing, I could hear a voice louder than all the rest crying out '*Rhowch Foliant*', and by and by another hollowing '*Rhowch Glod*', by this conduct . . . I concluded that these two persons might be seiz'd with a fit of the lunacy or frenzy. But as soon as this solemn part of the service was over Mr Rowland made a long extempore prayer before his sermon which prayer it seemed worked so upon most part of the audience that some cry'd out in one corner '*Rhowch Glod*', others in different parts of ye church bawled out as loud as possibly they could, '*Bendigedig, rhowch foliant*', and so on, that there was such a noise and confusion through the whole church that I had much ado, though I stood nigh the minister to make sense of anything he said. His preaching again flung almost the whole society into the greatest agitation and confusion possible, some cry'd, others laughed, ye women pulled one another by ye caps, embraced each other, caper'd like, where there was any room, but the perfectionists continued as before their huzzas. By this time poor me began to be uneasy too to see (I am sorry to say it) so much madness, so much irreverence, in the House of God . . . Nay I never saw greater instances of madness, even in *Bedlam* itself.

(An anonymous letter-writer, autumn 1746, in Theophilus Evans, *The History of Modern Enthusiasm*, London, 1752, p. 79.)

B.12   They are means of keeping up this same warmth and liveliness
that was ours at the beginning; as iron sharpeneth iron, so a man
sharpeneth the countenance of his friend. Fellowship is very
effective in stimulating us to good or evil; and what better
means of maintaining liveliness than to gather together to pray
together, to sing together and to declare the goodness of God to
one and another since the last meeting; relating the deliverances
of the Lord, revealing the way in which God has freed us from
the snare of the fowler, and how He has saved us from noisome
pestilence? God's people come away from such a meeting as this
like drunkards from the wine-shop — contentedly happy,
having drunk the wine of heaven; all comforted, guided and
edified. Some possibly, chastened in love, leaving the meeting
fully resolved to have done with their lusts; others weighted
down before the trials, discouragement and unbelief, now
strengthened in the faith . . . when Satan finds us one by one on
our own, he is more likely to intimidate us; but when the men of
God's army come together like this to talk about the powers of
heaven, and to tell how the keys of the bottomless pit are in the
possession of the Messiah . . . they gain new strength against
their spiritual enemies, the world, the flesh and the devil, and
part from each other confidently, cheerfully and courageously,
as those who had won the day.

(William Williams (Pantycelyn), *Drws y Society Profiad*, 1777,
translated by Mrs Martyn Lloyd Jones, *The Experience Meeting*,
Bridgend, 1973.)

B.13   It is a grand Mistake to teach poor Children their Duty in a
foreign Tongue, which takes up a good deal of time to little
purpose, for when they are employed for some time at the Plow
or Cart the language is lost, and they are so wise after five or six
Years Schooling as they were before, whereas were they taught
in their Mother's Tongue it would take but little time and
Charges. This method is as ridiculous and preposterous, as if
English Charity Boys should be instructed in Latin and Greek in
order to know their Duty.

(John Morgan, vicar of Matching, Essex, to Moses Williams,
13 May 1714, National Library of Wales MS 17B, p.12.)

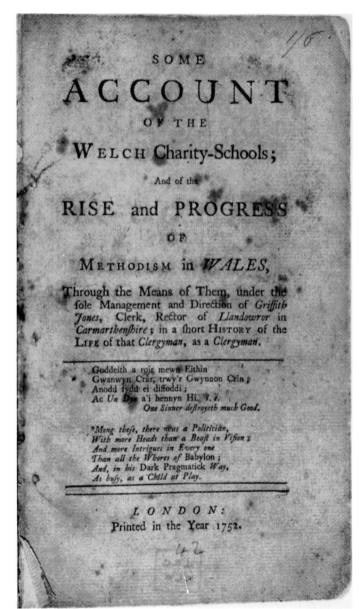

SOME

ACCOUNT

OF THE

WELCH Charity-Schools;

And of the

RISE and PROGRESS

OF

METHODISM in *WALES*,

Through the Means of Them, under the fole Management and Direction of *Griffith Jones*, Clerk, Rector of *Llandowror* in *Carmarthenfhire*; in a fhort HISTORY of the LIFE of that *Clergyman*, as a *Clergyman*.

> Goddeith a roir mewn Eithin
> Gwanwyn Crâs, trwy'r Gwynnon Crîn;
> Anodd fydd ei diffoddi;
> Ac *Un Dyn* a'i hennyn Hi. *T. J.*
>   *One Sinner deftroyeth much Good.*

> *'Mong thefe, there was a Politician,*
> *With more Heads than a Beaft in Vifion;*
> *And more Intrigues in Every one*
> *Than all the Whores of Babylon;*
> *And, in his Dark Pragmatick Way,*
> *As bufy, as a Child at Play.*

LONDON:
Printed in the Year 1752.

Title page of John Evans's *Some Account of the Welch Charity Schools*. (*Source: National Library of Wales.*)

B.14   What Length of Time, I may well ask, how many hundred
Years, must be allowed for the general Attainment of the
English, and the dying away of the Welsh Language? which has
hitherto survived some Thousands: And, in the mean time
while this is a doing (whether now or hereafter) what Myriads
of poor ignorant Souls must launch forth into the dreadful
Abyss of Eternity, and perish for want of Knowledge? and who
will answer for this?

.... our Language is so great a Protection and Defence to our
common People against the growing Corruption of the Times
in the English Tongue . . . Welsh is still the vulgar Tongue, and
not English. The English Charity-Schools, which have been
tried, produced no better effect in Country Places; all that the
Children could do in three, or four, or five Years amounted
commonly to no more than to learn very imperfectly to read
some easy Parts of the Bible, without knowing the Welsh of it,
nor the meaning of what they said when they repeated their
Catechism . . .

. . . Upon the Whole, it is humbly hoped, the Welsh
Language can be charged with no Blemishes, but such as may
serve to shew forth her Excellencies; and although now greatly
reduced in Estate, having been the Language of much larger
Territories, and at present contracted to a narrow Compass, She
has not lost her Charms, nor Chasteness, remains unalterably
the same, is now perhaps the same She was Four thousand Years
ago; still retains the Beauties of her Youth, grown old in Years,
but not decayed.

(Griffith Jones, *Welch Piety*, London, 1740, pp.32, 39, 44, 50–1.)

B.15   In a short Time after the School was opened, I went to visit it,
and was agreeably surprized to see there an Old Man seventy
one Years of Age, with his Spectacles on his Nose, and the
Church *Catechism* in his Hand, with five other poor People far
advanced in Years, who came there with their little Children to
be taught to read the Word of God. . . . I could not help being
much affected, I own, not only in hearing the poor Children
giving such an Account of the Principles of our holy Religion,
and of their Duty to God and Man, but likewise in observing

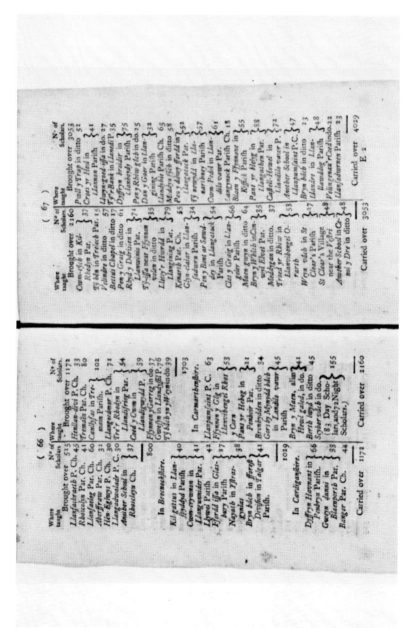

Griffith Jones's tables of schools and scholars in *Welch Piety*, 1759. (*Source: National Library of Wales.*)

the Congregation so attentive, and the Tears trickling down from their Eyes, when they saw that the little Children had gained more knowledge in three months at the Welch School, than many of them had acquired in hearing Sermons for fifty or threescore Years.

(Benjamin Morgans, vicar of Trelech, to Griffith Jones, 14 March 1754, in Griffith Jones, *Welch Piety*, London, 1755, pp.30–1.)

B.16   Schools and Scholars in Carmarthenshire, 1759 Llanpumsaint P.C. 63
Ffynnon y Gog in Llanvihengel Rhos y Corn 53
Pant yr Hebog in Penboir Par. 21
Bronhydden in ditto 34
Gors by Mynydd bach in Landilo vawr Parish 45
Bryn y Maen, alias Hewl galed, in do. 41
Berth lwyd in ditto 45
Scybor vach in do. (83 Day Scholars, and 72 Night Scholars) 155
Cwm-cych in Kilrhedyn Par. 37
Ty hen in Trelech Par. 15
Velindre in ditto 57

(Griffith Jones, *Welch Piety*, London, 1759, pp.66–7.)

B.17   The Benefit that our Neighbourhood received this last Quarter from the Welch School, incites us to bless God, and to return you our hearty Thanks, praying God to reward all the Promoters of so needful a Charity. I make bold to acquaint you that M R the Schoolmaster at present in Llandissilio Parish has used his utmost Diligence in a very engaging and familiar Way, to draw People of all Ages to be taught with Delight and Pleasure: in this Manner the Young and the Old have reaped uncommon Benefit in so small a Time. When the Parents and other Labourers, and indeed many Farmers, saw the Children so well instructed in the Principles of the Christian Religion, then they, who were of riper Years flocked there by Night, with their Candles and Fuels, desiring with great Concern to be likewise instructed. And I own, we, who were Standers by, had no small

A cartoon of 1763 portraying Methodist preachers as greedy men and their congregations as lewd and disorderly. (*Source: British Museum.*)

Pleasure and Satisfaction in seeing the Willingness of the Master to teach them, together with the Willingess of the Neighbourhood to be taught by him. I therefore pray God to prosper and increase the Number of faithful Schoolmasters.

(Watkin Watkins, gent., Llandysiliogogo, to Griffith Jones, 4 February 1758, in Griffith Jones, *Welch Piety*, London, 1758, pp.30–1.)

B.18   These South Wales, Enthusiastick Itinerants pretend to be Church of England people, and come to the Church; but at Nights they creep into such Houses, as they are able to work to themselves a Way to, and there delude ignorant Men and lead Captive silly Women and Children, by despising the Clergy, and accusing them of not preaching the Truth of the Gospel; assuring their Hearers that We are all Dumb Dogs, Blind Guides, False Prophets, Hirelings . . . But that they, and none others, are the Elect, the Chosen of God, the Predestinated, the Regenerated — that they cannot Sin in their Regenerate State . . . They promise Heaven to their Followers; and . . . damn all others, in order to terrify the Illiterate into their Faction. They assure them that their Fathers and Grand-Fathers are in Hell; and that they see the visible Marks of DAMNATION in the Faces of such as will not become *Methodists*.

(John Owen, chancellor of Bangor, to Griffith Jones, Llanddowror, 2 July 1743, in John Evans, *Some Account of the Welch Charity-Schools*, London, 1752, pp.86–7.)

B.19   O ye Maids of Roose, Judge between me and the Bishops and parsons. They are fat in Body, but Lean in Spirit. I am Lean in Body but Fat in Spirit. I have fed upon ye word till I am Increased to a great Bulk of Spirit. They have Fed upon Beef & Trolley till they are of Great Bulk of Body. . . . The Lambs of the Lord are willing to play, They are Beautiful to the Eye, They have velvet Thighs, Their Skins are soft, Their wool is white Like Cotton . . . I give you Leave to lay, my Lovely Lambs; Receive the Spirit within you with eagerness and Love; Dance and Skip about, for I will absolve you from your Sins, But whatever you do, Do in the dark, that our enemies may not triumph over us, for the eyes of the wicked Peep into every Corner.

(Lewis Morris, 'Young Mends the Clothier's Sermon', National
Library of Wales MS 67A, pp.57–68.)

B.20   The *Methodists* after having kept quiet for several years have of
late been very active. Their Number increases, and their wild
Pranks are beyond Description. The worship of the Day being
over, they have kept together in ye Place whole Nights, singing,
capering, bawling, fainting, thumping and a variety of other
Exercises. The whole Country for many Miles round have
crowded to see such strange Sights.

(David Lloyd, Brynllefrith, to the Revd Posthumus Lloyd,
Coventry, 27 April 1764, in George Eyre Evans (ed.), *Lloyd
Letters (1754–1796)*, Aberystwyth, 1908.)

B.21   The Enthusiasm of the *Methodists* together with the tyranny of
the Landowners have spread an universal gloom over the
country.

(William Jones, Llangadfan, to Edward Jones, 23 June 1789,
National Library of Wales MS 168, pp.297–8.)

Debating the Evidence

Every kind of source material presents difficulties of interpretation, but
sources of a religious nature are more difficult than most. If these
documents are *primary* sources — in the sense that they are contemporary with the events and persons mentioned — what exactly can
they tell us about the movement called *Methodism*? The complex
motives, the strongly-held views, the psychology of the individual and
of the crowd, are all here revealed or implicit, but the quantity of solid
fact is rather limited. A further problem is the reader's own set of
preconceptions; is one's response to these extracts inevitably coloured
by one's own view of religion?

    The following mixture of comment to ponder and questions to
answer about each of the sources is intended partly as an aid to
comprehension of the content of the documents, and partly as a stimulus

to thought abou: the nature and purpose of the documents and the
intention of their authors.

Source B.1
Williams Pantycelyn's view of religion in Wales before the *Methodist*
Revival (repeated in that well-known verse in his elegy to Howel Harris
in 1773: 'Pan oedd Cymru gynt yn gorwedd . . .' ('When Wales formerly
was supine . . .') became the generally accepted view of nineteenth-
century writers upon Welsh history. Does it accord with what is now
known of the Anglican and *Dissenting* churches before 1735? Does it, in
fact, exaggerate the impact that *Methodism* had on Wales?

Sources B.2 and B.3
These extracts suggest that, although they had little knowledge of
religion (as the *Methodists* understood it), the people of Wales were
eager, 'indeed ripe' for the Gospel. Did the *Methodists* in fact reap the
harvest carefully sown by previous generations of pious clergy and
Dissenting ministers?

Sources B.4 and B.6
Evan Evans (known either as Ieuan Fardd or Ieuan Brydydd Hir) was an
Anglican clergyman and also one of the best Welsh poets and scholars of
his time; he had become embittered by his lack of preferment in the
Church (he was never more than a curate). He lived in the neighbour-
hood of Llangeitho, the Cardiganshire headquarters of Daniel Rowland.
Are the two principal explanations of the success of the *Methodists* which
Evans puts forward in these two extracts, and in his picture of the state
of the Church in south Wales, an altogether adequate explanation of the
rise of *Methodism*?

Source B.5
An Englishman, Dr Thomas Bowles, was appointed rector of Trefdraeth and Llangwyfan in Anglesey in 1776. Only five of his 500
parishioners could speak English, and he was sued by his churchwardens and parishioners. With the financial support of prominent
people in Wales and in London, they successfully proved their parson's
unfitness for office on account of his ignorance of the Welsh language.
Dr Bowles's defence, quoted here, is an extreme assertion of the lack of
status of the language.

Source B.7

The first problem encountered by the reader of the voluminous diaries of Howel Harris is one of simply understanding what Harris is trying to say; his speed of writing and torrent of words often make the exact meaning obscure. Attempt a modern English paraphrase of the extract so that it becomes clearer how Howel Harris spent 10th May 1742. You will need to realize that the two sentences following 'NB' are in parenthesis — they are thoughts prompted by the news that he might be arrested 'by a gent'. 'Discoursed to 7' means 'until 7 o'clock', not 'to 7 persons'. Why do you think Harris (like several other *Methodist* leaders, such as the Wesleys) kept a diary from soon after his conversion in 1735 to within a short time of his death in 1773? (In answering you will need to think about the mixture of fact and religious feeling which he recorded daily.)

Sources B.8 and B.10

These are descriptions of Howel Harris and Daniel Rowland written by fellow *Methodists*. Contrast them with the hostile passages in Sources B.9 and B.11. Does what *Wesley* wrote constitute evidence which a historian can make use of?

Sources B.9 and B.11

Allowing for the hostility of these writers towards Enthusiasm (*Theophilus Evans* provides a classic example), can we accept their accounts as, in essence, truthful? (Remember that Evans is speaking generally, while the anonymous writer is apparently giving an eye-witness's account of a particular occasion).

Source B.12

Contrast Pantycelyn's sober and idealized account of a society meeting (*seiat*) with what is said in Sources B.9 and B.11. Note that a society meeting was not a preaching service; what, in fact, were the essential differences between them?

Sources B.13 and B.14

Why did John Morgan and Griffith Jones think it essential that the language used in schools should be Welsh? Compare their attitude to the language with that of Dr Bowles in Source B.5.

Sources B.14 and B.17
What can be learnt from these extracts about the curriculum of the *circulating schools?*

Source B.18
What was the nub of this prominent Anglican clergyman's complaint to Griffith Jones? (The 'Enthusiastic Itinerants' complained of were the teachers of the *circulating schools*.)

Source B.19
This is clearly a satire, a parody of a *Methodist* sermon, but can we learn anything from such innuendos as *Lewis Morris* indulges in? Maybe not all *Methodist* emotionalism was purely spiritual — this is what he hints. Clearly this is not *evidence* (it is mischievous, or even malicious, libel); but it puts us on our guard against accepting too readily the 'holier-than-thou' stance of the Enthusiasts.

Source B.20
Source B.9 and B.11 were hostile descriptions of enthusiasts written in the 1740s and 1750s by Anglicans. This is an account written by a very distinguished *Dissenter*, David Lloyd, minister of Llwynrhydowen chapel in the Vale of Teifi, Cardiganshire, in the 1760s. Is there any significant difference between the picture presented in these three accounts?

Source B.21
Link this remark by *William Jones* of Llangadfan with Gwyn A. Williams's chapter 'Beginnings of Radicalism'.

Discussion

Geraint Jenkins has made a selection of documents which illustrates the spectrum of attitudes and opinions — those of leading *Methodists* (Enthusiasts) themselves (B.1, B.3, B.7, B.8, B.10, B.12) and their sympathizers, and those of their opponents among the traditionalist Anglican clergy and laity (B.4, B.6, B.9, B.11, B.18, B.19), the *Dissenting* ministry (B.20) and late eighteenth-century radicals (B.21).

With religious history we are partly in the realm of ideas — what

The First Methodist Association (*Sasiwn*) in 1743. (*Source: National Library of Wales.*)

people thought and believed — and partly in the more tractable world of fact, of events, of what happened. The problem for the historian who must approach these two aspects or levels of religious history is that so much of the voluminous contemporary documentation contains little by way of verifiable fact but a great deal of opinion, often expressed with unrestrained passion. In a word, the sources are tendentious; they are calculated to persuade rather than to inform. Few things raised such strong emotions in the eighteenth century as did 'Enthusiasm'. The clash of opinions — if understood for what it is — can, however, leave the reader with a vivid impression of the nature and character of *Methodism* and *Methodists*, and it is this impression which Dr Jenkins intends that his readers shall gain.

The reader may be left with little idea of the 'facts' or realities of eighteenth-century *Methodism*. For example, the growth and spread of *Methodism* after 1735 was slow and fitful, for reasons which the historian can attempt to expound — not making a real 'breakthrough' in many parts of Wales until the early decades of the nineteenth century. But contemporary *Methodist* writing gives little direct information about this. As far as *Methodists* were concerned we are perhaps to understand that the conversions of 1735 were the only historical events that mattered; they simply contrasted the religious destitution of the country before 1735 with its privileged state thereafter (B.1). *Methodists* were concerned with spiritual things — dates, causes, quantities, trends belong in the vocabulary of social historians not of enthusiasts. An eighteenth-century *Methodist* would not try to explain the movement in the way that a modern historian would seek to do — to him events were not the result of antecedent causes but of God's purpose for the world.

Nevertheless, some of the documents (notably B.4 and B.6) do present an historical explanation of the phenomenon of *Methodism*, as understood by a disgruntled Anglican curate. And some facts are recorded in addition to his own thoughts by Howel Harris in his diary (B.7). The factual record of *circulating schools* held was published annually by the meticulous Griffith Jones (B.16). But by far the greater part of the documents are of a quite different kind, deliberately chosen by Dr Jenkins to reflect the tone of contemporary writing. Such metaphors as 'What a nursing- father has God sent us!' (B.8) are representative — the influence of Biblical prose is pervasive — and we need to gain experience in how to evaluate, and how to extract historical information from, such outpourings.

Engraving showing an iron forge between Dolgellau and Barmouth, 1776. (*Source: National Library of Wales.*)

The Quickenings of Industrial Activity

R.O. ROBERTS

The title of this essay points immediately to a number of considerations. In the first place, the word 'quickenings' leads to the reflection that, overall, what happened in Wales in the eighteenth century was an acceleration of previous developments rather than an absolute beginning, though there were in certain pursuits and in some places such beginnings — that is, quickenings in the other sense of 'coming to life'. (This touches, of course, upon the questions about the meaning and applicability in this field of terms like 'industrial evolution', 'industrial revolution' and 'take-off'.) Secondly, the word 'quickenings', in the plural, reminds us of the fact that in Wales there were very many small industrial establishments of seventeenth-century origin, dispersed over much of the country, whose output increased appreciably. Thirdly, the adjective 'industrial' calls for comment. Economists define an industry as a collection of establishments (that is, works) or of firms specializing in making the same category of product(s), largely to the exclusion of other establishments or firms. And clearly, by such definition, agriculture, fishing and the provision of various services are industries. However, attention is here confined to mining, quarrying and manufacturing — a group of industries which in fact probably accounted for fewer than a sixth of Welsh occupied jobs throughout the eighteenth century.

The available resources on which these industries could draw before the nineteenth century were the small and thinly dispersed population (which was growing fairly slowly), the land and the produce of its farms, stone and minerals of various kinds, a plentiful supply of water, a coastline with numerous creeks and harbours, and a few stretches of inland navigable waters. By around 1700 various industrial activities in Wales were already well established, some of them being centuries old. Indeed, in the story of quarrying and mining, rural crafts and manufacture (that is, producing by hand — the word deriving from the Latin *manu*, 'by hand', and *facere*, 'to make'), no sharp break occurred at the beginning of the eighteenth century. Already, by the close of the previous century the production of woollen and leather goods, the making of buildings and articles of wood, stone, metal and clay, the smelting of ferrous and non-ferrous metal ores and the milling of cereals had developed significantly. Woollen manufacture — long established as the largest industry other than the farming of which it was an adjunct — was widespread throughout country districts but with main concentrations in the historic counties of Montgomery, Merioneth and Denbigh. But such quickenings as took place in the seventeenth century appear to have occurred mainly in mining and in the production of metals, for which there were growing demands for civil and military uses.

More especially in areas near navigable waters (notably in north-east Wales, south Pembrokeshire, south-east Carmarthenshire and west Glamorgan), coal came to be dug from levels and, in some places, even from mines deep enough to warrant installation of various devices for removing water and also of primitive procedures for dealing with gas. But, between 1650 and 1700, even the deeper coal seams of the relatively landlocked areas of mid-Glamorgan and Monmouthshire were being tapped — a development which has been regarded as 'perhaps the most significant' of that half-century in southern Wales.[1] In the metal industries, from the late sixteenth century in Cardiganshire and from the early seventeenth century in Flintshire and Denbighshire, there was mining and smelting of lead-silver ores; further expansion of this industry followed the interruption of its activity during the mid-seventeenth-century political upheavals and *Civil War*. Technology in lead smelting was developing so fast — beyond the crude 'boles', that is primitive smelting hearths[2] — that in 1667 at one smelting site employing twenty-one men immediately south of the Dyfi estuary, there were five ore-hearths 'with backs, cheeks, work stones, iron plates and other necessaries' with 'five pairs of large smelting bellows . . . one new large water wheel', an 'old Mint House', stamping mills, a refining mill, a red-lead mill, and much else.[3] Furthermore, iron furnaces and forges were dispersed over much of the country. Having been prohibited from obtaining charcoal from the timber of the *Weald* district, Sussex ironmasters from the 1560s onwards set up small, charcoal-burning blast-furnaces in Glamorgan and Monmouthshire; industrial archaeologists have located the sites of twenty early furnaces and five associated forges in the two counties. In the seventeenth century similar iron furnaces and forges were set up in rural districts in Carmarthenshire, Cardiganshire, Pembrokeshire and Denbighshire. And in various parts of Wales the production of charcoal for the metal works has been described as a 'highly organised' industry.[4] Overall, however, in Britain during the seventeenth century, and particularly between the 1630s and 1680s, there was what has been called a 'dynamic shortage' of charcoal for fuelling iron furnaces and forges — a shortfall described as 'dynamic' because large increases in the demand for home-produced iron (and hence for charcoal) outstripped the supplies.[5] And, towards the close of the century, the persisting exigencies of providing fuel and other requisites for the metal industries, and of making the latter more efficient, called for a continuation, if not an intensification, of the searchings and adaptations of earlier decades. These were to yield striking results.

For the further quickenings of industrial activity during the eighteenth century, Wales could draw on the resources already mentioned — land, minerals, water, harbours and, most important, its population (which was continuing to grow). There were, however, some serious hindrances to the development of mining and manufacture. Clearly, the demand for such industrial products as Wales could effectively produce was constricted by the small size and low incomes of its population and that of other places within trading reach. With regard to the supply of commodities, the same smallness of the Welsh population and its dispersion limited the availability in potential locations for industry of the three 'factors of production' — enterprise (or entrepreneurship), capital and labour.

Coal staithe and a copper works at Landore, near Swansea, 1792, a watercolour by J.C. Ibbetson. (*Source: The Wernher Collection, Luton.*)

Potential entrepreneurs — those who took the major business decisions and the major risks — were only a very small proportion of the population; the same was true of those who supplied loan capital. Even the landowners and others who could have set up and developed industrial enterprises were

C.1   sometimes loath to do so (C.1, C.2). Furthermore, the number

C.2   of labourers residing within easy reach of any particular works was usually small. Now, the phrase 'within easy reach' reminds one of the major hindrance to industrial growth in eighteenth-century Wales, namely the very rudimentary means of overland

C.3   transport by bridle-path and pot-holed tracks (C.3). This rendered the movement of heavy and bulky raw materials and finished products very costly — sometimes, as in the case of

C.4a   some unexploited coal resources, prohibitively so (C.4a, C.4b,

C.4b   C.4c, C.5). But, of course, the smallness of scale of economic

C.4c   activity in various inland areas itself inhibited the provision of

C.5   better facilities: the retarding influences interacted. There are a few examples of pit coal and limestone actually being moved at a cost higher than the total of all the other charges of supplying these products. Again, in the first half of the eighteenth century, upwards of a quarter and even a third of the cost of charcoal supplied at smelting furnaces was incurred by transport charges. In fact, the continuing shortages of this fuel meant that — despite the deterioration due to its fragility — it had often to be brought to the furnaces and to the forges from distant woods and coppices: for example, it was carried from the upper Taff Valley to the Caerphilly furnace in Glamorgan and to the Machen forge in Monmouthshire, and from as far as Llangamarch and Llanwrtyd to the Brecon furnace. So, on account of both the difficulties of supplying it and the strength of the demand for it, charcoal could be the major cost item in the production of iron: thus in the Clydach furnace in Breconshire in 1704 no less than six-sevenths of the cost of making pig iron arose from purchasing charcoal.

The hindrances mentioned, however, were far from overwhelming. Inducements to overcome the difficulties were strong enough in certain circumstances to allow new developments to be undertaken. Though the total demand for industrial products was small, that for certain goods at particular times

Token coin of the ironworks of Carmarthen and Cwmdwyfran in the late eighteenth century, showing the tapping of the furnace and the forging into bar iron. (*Source: Carmarthen Museum.*)

could be strong: sometimes, for example, conditions of war or
C.6 the expectation of hostilities had this effect (C.6). And an
appreciable extension of demand for a product could come
about following a lowering of price which, in turn, might be the
result of improvement in the technique of production. Where
both demand and supply conditions seemed promising, there
were entrepreneurs anxious to bring together workers and
capital and to undertake production. Some prominent business
leaders came from outside Wales, and not all native entrepreneurs eschewed industrial ventures: landowners like the
Vaughans of Golden Grove, Carmarthenshire, the Mansells of
west Glamorgan and the Hughes of Anglesey were ready
supporters of schemes which provided a market for the timber
or minerals of their estates. Enterprise was stimulated by the
intermittent discoveries of new sources of iron ore and coal, by
the finding of rich veins of lead in Cardiganshire between 1740
and 1752, and the discovery of the rich copper ore of north
Anglesey in 1761. When economic prospects became sufficiently auspicious in certain inland districts — as happened
from the 1750s onwards — entrepreneurs initiated important
developments to overcome the lack of transport facilities:
existing tracks were improved and canals were cut — the latter,
first and modestly, in the coastal district near Llanelli, Carmarthenshire, to be followed by the twenty to thirty-mile-long
canals of the eastern and western valleys of the southern coalfield. Capital was supplied fairly readily by local landowners and
by industrialists and traders from England. Population growth,
especially towards the close of the century, together with the
prospects of higher wages, made it possible to recruit unskilled
workers from the regions of the works and to attract skilled
workers and managers from much further afield — Cornish
C.7 miners to Cardiganshire and Anglesey, for example (C.7).

Notable among the technological developments which
stimulated enterprise were the remarkable advances in the
methods of producing metals. In the Bristol area in the late
seventeenth century a satisfactory method was developed for
smelting lead, copper and tin 'in close or *reverberatory furnaces*
with pitt coals or sea coals . . .'[6] Again, as is well known,
Abraham Darby at Coalbrookdale, Shropshire succeeded

between 1709 and 1718 in smelting iron ore with coke — the residue from coal after the removal of volatile constituents. And the processes of refining pig iron into bar iron were greatly improved by the invention of the 'potting method' in the early 1760s and then much further advanced by Henry Cort's *'puddling process'* patented in 1783–4. In addition, by the mid-century, more powerful steam-powered (and thus more controllable) blast mechanisms became available to allow furnaces to derive economies of larger scale. The application of steam power also had crucial effects on the mining industries. Newcomen's 'atmospheric engine', devised in 1705, was to be widely used for powering pumps to remove water out of mines; and James Watt's improved steam engine of 1769 was to be employed — among other uses — in moving workers and materials up and down mine shafts.

It was these influences which explain the main industrial quickenings in Wales during the eighteenth century, for example, in the woollen industry. Around the middle of the century the industry had experienced a modest expansion of activity in its main producing region of Montgomery, Merioneth and south Denbighshire: new outlets and marketing procedures were then arranged for the produce of Montgomeryshire. But it was not until the last decade of the century that a major quickening came to the industry in that county: new mills with water-driven machinery were set up, and the tourist Arthur Aikin, in 1797, even concluded that the flannel industry was 'the grand and most important of Welsh manufactures'[7] (C.8).

C.8

In the case of non-ferrous metals there were important responses in Wales both to the strong demand for copper, lead and zinc, and their alloys, and also to innovations in extracting and smelting the ores (C.9). It is true that in the first few decades of the century the quickenings in mining for lead-silver ores in Cardiganshire were much more discernible in expectation, investment and effort than in output, but the major discoveries of such ores — successively at Darren, Cwmsymlog and Esgair-mwyn in 1740–52 — brought about a successful burst of activity until decline set in from the 1770s onwards. In Flintshire, on the other hand, the mining for lead — and calamine (zinc ore) was also raised — appears to have been

C.9

rather more continuously successful than in Cardiganshire during the century. There were also vigorous searches for copper ore which came to concentrate particularly upon Parys Mountain in north Anglesey where, in 1768, a large quantity of high quality mineral was found. Extraction followed immediately and on a substantial scale: in the highly productive and profitable opencast area and the nearby mine, 1,200 workers were employed during the 1780s, which was the peak decade of activity; and the output (in terms of metal content) was over a third of that of Britain — which was then the world's largest producer of copper (C.10). The very brief bonanza period enabled one of Europe's foremost entrepreneurs — Thomas Williams, the 'Copper King', of Llanidan — to extend the mining firms' activities from Anglesey into smelting, manufacturing and marketing copper in Flintshire, Lancashire, west Glamorgan, London, Birmingham and elsewhere.

C.10

For taking advantage of the revolutionary method of smelting non-ferrous metals, innovated in the Bristol area, only one area in Wales was sufficiently favoured with local supplies of the ores and of coal, together with the added major advantage of nearness to navigable water. This was that part of Flintshire close to the Dee estuary where, in the Bagillt area, what was claimed to be improved coal-burning, *reverberatory furnaces* came into use for smelting lead from 1704 onwards. To such smelteries in Flintshire throughout the century there came not only the produce of nearby mines but also some of the lead ores of Cardiganshire and elsewhere, which were also sent to the western parts of the main south Wales coalfield. In the latter area the coal measures reach down to the coast, thus providing a highly attractive location for smelting establishments — an attraction which some landowners in the area strengthened by the highly modern device of offering initial incentives to potential incoming partnerships (C.11). In the technology in use at the time, smelting non-ferrous metal ores involved using coal and ore in a ratio by weight of about 3:1, and so the ores, especially those of copper from Cornwall, Anglesey and a few other places, were brought by sea to new works in the Swansea region. Thus it was that, immediately following the Bristol discoveries, works for smelting copper and lead were set up —

C.11

The Parys Copper Mine, Anglesey, *c.* 1785, a watercolour by J.C. Ibbetson. (*Source: National Museum of Wales.*)

from the 1690s in the Neath area and from 1717 in the lower Tawe Valley near Swansea. Though they employed no more than about 200 persons in 1740 and about 500 in 1780, they gave employment to many others (possibly also around 500 by the latter date) in collieries and in the provision of transport and various services. They accounted for about half of Britain's copper-smelting capacity in the 1750s and some ninety per cent by the 1790s.

Despite small local advances it was not until the second half of the century that a real quickening of activity occurred in the iron industry. Unlike the immediate spread of new methods of smelting lead and copper, the diffusion of the Coalbrookdale invention of 1709–18 had to wait for around fifty years; and the main advance in the method of processing pig into bar iron came still later, towards the close of the century.

For much of the period the smelting of iron was done in charcoal-fired, water-powered, blast furnaces. The resulting pig iron was either made into bar iron in charcoal-fuelled and water-driven forges (steam power being also used in the last quarter of the century) or it was cast into hardware in foundries. Each of the largest of these establishments, such as those of Clydach and Pontypool, normally yielded at most a few hundred tons annually: the few works in Montgomery and Merioneth produced only up to about ten tons a year, largely for local use. Minor quickenings of activity were experienced in a few localities as entrepreneurs from England came to exploit newly discovered sources of ore and charcoal; and at the Bersham Works near Wrexham there was, in the 1720s, a short-lived attempt to smelt with coke.

The diffusion into Wales of the Coalbrookdale method of smelting began in Bersham in the 1750s and continued on a larger scale between 1757 and 1789 in new works along the north-eastern rim of the coalfield in Glamorgan and Monmouthshire. This area was favoured with its own resources of iron ore, coal, limestone, refractory materials and water. The smelting establishments here were those of Hirwaun and of Dowlais followed by the Plymouth, Cyfarthfa and Penydarren works in the Merthyr area and, to the east, the Tredegar, Sirhowy, Beaufort and Blaenavon works (C.12a, C.12b). These

C.12a

87

C.12b   enterprises adopted — and in some cases improved upon — new methods of casting or forging their pig iron. At Bersham under the Wilkinsons, in the second half of the century, the production of cylindrical and other castings was enlarged and
C.13   became more efficient (C.13). And for the production of wrought iron the 'potting' method was introduced in the middle 1760s at Cyfarthfa where improvements were later made to the process. This technique involved re-melting coke-smelted 'pigs' and re-heating the resulting de-siliconized iron, along with a flux, in crucibles or 'pots' in coal-fired *reverberatory furnaces*.[8] The method appears to have been adopted by most British iron firms by the late 1780s, when the more well-known *'puddling process'* came to be adopted in Welsh works as in others.

    Tin-plate manufacture grew in south Wales as an important appendage of the iron industry. In Pontypool around 1690, John Hanbury developed a commercially viable method of rolling iron into sheets and thinly coating their surfaces with tin. During the first half of the following century the demand within Britain for this product remained fairly modest and constant — it was being used increasingly instead of pewter. From the mid-century, output grew as sales increased as a result of price reductions and interruption of German supplies during the War of Austrian Succession. And so, from 1749 onwards, a number of small tin-plate works was set up in south Wales — between Llechryd, Cardiganshire in the west and Caerleon, Monmouthshire in the east — so that by the beginning of the nineteenth century most of the fourteen tin-plate works in Britain were
C.14   located in the region (C.14).

    Underpinning the industrial developments which have been mentioned — and also depending largely upon them — was the coal industry. The latter grew in Wales during the eighteenth century as a result of entrepreneurial response to demands from metal production and other industries and from households
C.15   within and outside the country (C.15). This response became more effective, but at the cost of very great human sacrifice, with increasing knowledge of the coal resources available and of improved methods of dealing with the problems presented by transportation and by water and dangerous gases underground: water adits, ventilation shafts, pumps powered by water, horse

and steam, and water-balances were brought into use over the
C.16 years (C.16). Furthermore, as previously indicated, colliery
development depended largely upon access to market; and it
was the nearness of a number of collieries to Swansea and its
subsidiary ports that largely explains the roughly fifty-per-cent
increase in the annual shipment of coal from south Wales during
the first half of the eighteenth century. By the end of the century
the yearly tonnage of coal which left Swansea alone was about
double the mid-century annual shipment from the whole of
south Wales (including the Pembrokeshire collieries). And
industrial and domestic consumption of coal within the region
also grew rapidly. Access to ports, however, did not always lead
to a significant increase in shipments. Thus, despite such an
advantage, in the Llanelli area the only period of marked
expansion in coal output was the 1750s and 1760s — the
suggested explanation being lack of entrepreneurship other
than in those two decades.[9] Again, despite the facilities of
Deeside, the expansion of the coal industry in north-east Wales
appears to have been more dependent on its own region's
industrial demand, and less dependent upon shipment, than was
that of its larger south Wales counterpart.

The final industry mentioned here is that of slate production.
In the middle decades of the eighteenth century there was a
growing demand for roofing slates which led to a modest
increase in the number and the output of shallow excavations in
the counties of Caernarfon and Merioneth. By the 1770s perhaps
around fifty partners were engaged in a group of such workings
near Llyn Padarn and Llyn Peris in the hinterland of the port of
Caernarfon; and north-east of this area — near what later came
to be the township of Bethesda — similar partnerships were
granted leases for quarrying, albeit without much resulting
output. Soon after this, however, in the 1780s and early 1790s,
vigorous entrepreneurship and management of estates immediately south-east of Bangor and of Caernarfon brought a
consolidation of leases and much more active quarrying for, and
trading in, slate. About seven million slates of various kinds
were shipped annually from Caernarfon and creeks near Bangor
in the early 1790s; and employment in the two clusters of
quarries — near Llanberis and Bethesda — had rapidly grown

Penrhyn Slate Quarry in 1808. (Source: Gwynedd Archives Service.)

C.17 to about 1,000 men (C.17). These two groups then accounted for some sixty per cent of the slate output of Wales, the other main quarrying districts being south of Caernarfon in the Nantlle, Beddgelert and Ffestiniog areas. The burst of slate-producing activity, however, was sharply interrupted by the sudden reduction of building work consequent upon the war with France from 1793 onwards, and the imposition of a heavy, war-induced, tax on roofing slates. It was not until the next century that the industry resumed its expansion, but the rapid growth of the 1780s and early 1790s had been full of promise.

Indeed, the quickenings during the eighteenth century in the various other industries which have been briefly discussed in this essay were also more significant as promise than achievement. They provided the beginnings of later — and often spectacular — development.

Notes

1 William Rees, *Industry before the Industrial Revolution*, Cardiff, 1968, Vol.I, p.291.
2 See ibid., Vol.I, p.165; and *A New English Dictionary*, Vol.I, Oxford 1888, p.972.
3 Rees, op.cit., Vol.II, p.579; *Historical Metallurgy*, Vol.XX, no.2, 1986, p.66.
4 Rees, op.cit., Vol.I, p.291.
5 See Brinley Thomas, 'Was there an energy crisis in Great Britain in the 17th Century?', *Explorations in Economic History*, 23, 1986, pp.128–9ff.
6 From a description of Viscount Gradison's patent (Patent Specifications, no.206) in J.R. Harris, *The Copper King: A Biography of Thomas Williams of Llanidan*, Liverpool, 1964, p.3.
7 Arthur Aikin, *Journal of a Tour through North Wales*, 1797, p.73.
8 See Charles K. Hyde, *Technological Change and the British Iron Industry, 1700–1870*, New Jersey, 1977, p.83.
9 See M.V. Symons, *Coal Mining in the Llanelli Area*, Vol.I, Llanelli, 1979, pp.39–40.

Sources

C.1 ... I will tell you a word or two about Cardiganshire. This is the richest county I ever knew, & the one which contains the fewest clever or ingenious people. I know several persons as poor as John, Ben Clyttwr, who have veins of lead ore on their lands: &

The Darren Lead Mine, Cardiganshire, *c.* 1670. (*Source: Welsh Industrial and Maritime Museum.*)

yet they will neither work them themselves, nor suffer any other person to do so. I am as well convinced, as that I am in this place, that if some company were to advance me two hundred pounds, I could soon make two thousand of them: yes, & for aught I know, two thousand a year: and what is still more, a great probability of making twelve thousand a year. Who would not venture all one is worth? They have raised at Darren Vawr Hill, near Aberystwyth, for some years, 200 tons every quarter of a year, which is 800 ton per ann. The ore contains 50 to 60 ounces silver; some more, some less, & is worth clear on the bank or quay £20 a ton; & 20 × 800 = £16,000 a year. But the charge or expence to be deducted, is about £4,000. So there is a clear profit of £12,000 a year; & all within the compass of 200 yards . . .

(Lewis Morris of Anglesey to Williams Morris; from Kington, Herefordshire, February 11 [? 1742]. Hugh Owen (ed.), 'Additional Letters of the Morrises of Anglesey', *Y Cymmrodor*, Vol.XLIX, Part I, 1947, p.113.)

C.2   . . . a rich lead mine on the Estate of Captain Lloyd of Bronwydd, worked by Lord Milford about 7 years ago, but their lease expiring it was discontinued. Some partner [?] with Lord Milford formed a little company. The profits were believed to be great: the ore is said to be rich and abundant, but none have since thought it worth notice on the terms that it can be at present obtained. This is a very common case I find. The proprietor of the land [?] discovering that his mines has afforded some profit becomes exhorbitant in his demands from those who would carry on the working of them. On the other hand adventurers knowing the great hazards attending their speculations will not enter on them unless they can obtain leases or contracts that afford them a greater chance of profit, and that considerable, than of loss: they seldom meddle with cases that are doubtful. Thus are some of the richest mines in the country left unworked . . .

(Edward Williams, 'Accounts of Journeys', c.1800 [?]; the lead mine mentioned was at Llanfyrnach, Pembrokeshire. National Library of Wales MS 13156A.)

C.3   Large strings of horses are daily, almost hourly, seen in the
        summer season, conveying the oar to Caermarthen. It is carried
        in small baggs two upon a horse and deposited in the
        warehouses for that purpose, to be shipped from thence in
        sloops to the smelting houses.

(Richard C. Hoare, 'Journals of Tours in Wales', *c.*1776.
National Library of Wales MS 16988-9C.)

C.4a   The coals at a distance from Navigation were considered of no
        value, and the tenants were indulged in working a little coal for
        their own use, which they did by making small holes in the sides
        of the Hills; but even in doing this some of them were
        interrupted by his grace's agents at particular times . . .

(Statement by Gabriel Powell, the Duke of Beaufort's steward
for the Seigniories of Gower and Kilvey, dated 1747. Quoted
from 'Badminton Papers' in W.H. Jones, *History of the Port of
Swansea*, Carmarthen, 1922, p.339. Cf. a different attribution
with an incorrect date in A.H. John, *Industrial Development in
South Wales*, Cardiff, 1950, p.6.)

C.4b   There are under the commons and wastes within this manor
        ['Gower Supra boscus . . . or Welsh Gower'] several valuable
        mines, of coal and *culm* belonging to the Lord; but being at a
        distance from navigation the tenants have license granted them
        to work for their own use during the Lords' pleasure . . .

(Gabriel Powell, 'Survey of the Seigniories of Gower and
Kilvey . . . Made in the year 1764'. Transcribed in University
College of Swansea Library, Grant Francis Papers B4.)

C.4c   There are several veins or mines of coal wrought in this manor,
        ['The Seigniory . . . of Kilvey'] for which the Lord receives a
        customary payment of four pence a *wey* for every *wey* of coal
        ship'd to be exported over the Bar of Swansea each way [*sic*] to
        contain forty-eight bags and every bag twenty four Winchester
        Gallons . . .

(Gabriel Powell, op.cit.)

C.5   It is to be observed that slate being so heavy an article makes profit to the Adventurers very trifling so as not to be an object even when there is a great Demand for them as there is at present, unless great quantity can be raised and brought to the shipping place which cannot be done without first laying out a very considerable sum in clearing the Face of the rock and making New Roads and repairing others so as to reduce the Rate of Cost as much as possible; which for some time past before the new Undertaking had been estimated at or near half the value of the Countesses and always half the Value of the Ton Slate, Ladies and Doubles [sizes of slate], tho' at other Quarries the Tons etc. are carried for less than the third of their Value and the Countesses for about a fourth of the Value. The distance from the Upper Quarry to the Shipping Place is upwards of eight miles, and no road that a Cart can go upon within three miles of the Quarries . . .

(The comments of three slate-quarrying partners at Dinorwig, 4 February 1788. University College of North Wales Library, Porth yr Aur MS 29095, quoted in Jean Lindsay, *A History of the North Wales Slate Industry*, Newton Abbot and London, 1974, p.58.)

C.6   . . . to be sure tis to our Interest to reduce the Debt on the Dukes Mortgage by selling the Wood, most certain great care must be taken where an agreement is made as you know what kind of people we have to Deal with . . . As we are at the Eve of a War timber bears a good price . . .

(A letter from John Vaughan, Golden Grove Estate, Carmarthenshire, to his son, Richard, 21 February 1756. Carmarthenshire Record Office, Cawdor/Vaughan Papers 102/8029.)

C.7   The Man I agreed with when in Bristol does not Seem to turn out to our Expectation, therefore shall be obliged to you to agree with Absolum. And have to observe to you that we have altered the Plan of work so as to have three hands to work Eight hours shifts. Therefore on his Working an Eight hours shift and taking the care of the Engine upon him I will (on your recommendation of his Abilities), allow him the wages he wanted when I was in Bristol, which was 15/- per week, House, & Firing. If he approves on the Terms, could wish he would set out directly . . .

(Thomas Guest, 'Dowlais Furnace', to John Hawkins, 13 June 1785. Glamorgan Archive Service, Dowlais Iron Company 'Copy Letters 1782–94', p.174, quoted in M. Elsas (ed.), *Dowlais Iron Company Letters 1782–1860*, Cardiff, 1960, p.18.)

C.8 So immense is the wealth that flows into that town [Dolgellau] from the woollen manufactory and such are the consequences derived from it . . . that in Dolgelley alone no less than from £50,000 to £100,000 is annually returned in the article of coarse webs for soldier's cloathing.

(Account dated 1796 in the *Cambrian Register*. Quoted in M.J. Jones, 'Gwlanen Glannau'r Wnion', *Journal of the Merioneth Historical and Record Society*, Vol.VIII, 2, 1978, p.194.)

C.9 Though the upper regions of the Towy are less prolific upon the surface than the lower parts of the Vale . . . yet are they more prolific to the owner than if they were clothed with a profusion of Grain . . . in the Strata of the Earth have been discovered extensive veins of Lead.

Nine inexausted [*sic*] mines are work'd to great advantage. Besides the immense Profits arising from thence to Mr Cambel the proprietor they add add [*sic*] a richness to the barren district in which they lie. Employment is found for individuals who are collected for that purpose; habitations are built for their reception on convenient situations around, and an appearance of industry every where prevails.

(Richard C. Hoare, 'Journals of Tours in Wales', *c*.1796. National Library of Wales MS 169988-9C.)

C.10 . . . having taken a slight repast at Amlwch we proceeded to the Parys mountain which of late years has enriched not only many individuals but the nation at large . . . the approach to it is dreary in the extreme for the sulphurious steams issuing from

Copper works in the Greenfield Valley, near Holywell, Flintshire, 1792. *(Source: Clwyd Record Office.)*

the copper kilns have destroyed every germ of vegetation in the neighbourhood. When we had gained the higher ground the uninteresting and gloomy prospect we had hitherto observed was at once converted into the most lively and active scene. Hundreds of men women and children, appeared busily occupied in the different branches of this vast concern and the bustle of the metropolis prevailed amidst the dreary recesses of the Druids . . . we first were conducted to some wooden stages erected on the edge of an immense excavation of an oval form about two hundred yards long, half as much in width and eighty in depth which has been hollowed out in the course of twenty years . . . on looking down from hence to the chasm beneath, we saw the rock rich with ore of a light gold colour which the miners were busily engaged in boring, blasting, breaking with sledge hammers, wheeling the fragments to appointed places beneath the stages filling the baskets which were hauled up . . . by the windlass. There might be from twelve to fourteen stages erected for this purpose in different parts of the mine. As soon as the commodity is landed it is delivered to a number of women and children to be broken into smaller pieces, the good ore is then separated from that of an inferior sort and carried to kilns to be baked the sulphur forms in what is called flour brimstone . . . collected, melted in large cauldrons and formed into round moulds for sale. We understood that the better kind of ore was sent to Neath and other places, and the inferior to the smelting houses at Amlwch.

(Revd John Skinner, [Transcript of] 'A Ten Days Tour in Anglesea, 1802'. National Library of Wales MS 21031, fo.62.)

C.11   'Indenture of this date [21 March 1736] between the Honourable Bussy Mansel of Britton Ferry in the County of Glamorgan Esqre of the one part and Thomas Coster of the City of Bristol Esqre Joseph Percival and Samuel Percival of the same City Merchants & Henry Barne of the City of Bristol aforesaid Merchant [*the Partners*] of the other part' — setting out the terms of a lease from B. Mansel to the Partners for 51 years from Lady Day 1737 of lands 'known by the name of Craig Knap Loth [Craig Cnap Coch] and White Rock Coal place or Banks' etc. by the Tawe near Swansea.

These terms included the undertakings that *the Partners* 'would . . . within the space of 3 years . . . build and set up on the said demised premises one new Copper Smelting house or Workhouse for smelting making or refining Coper or any other Metals and to contain 20 furnaces at least with such warehouses Mills and other Buildings as they the said . . . [Partners] . . . should judge necessary and convenient . . .

. . . That they would not at any time during the s^d Term alien assign or dispose of the said premises to any person or persons who should at that time be concerned or interested in any . . . Copper Works situate on the Rivers of Swansea or Neath without the license of the s^d Bussy Mansel his heirs & assigns first obtained . . . That the s^d Bussy Mansel in consideration of the s^d buildings so to be erected and towards carrying on the same and to make up the s^d sum of £1400 before covenanted so to be expended in and about the same sho^d pay unto the said . . . [Partners] . . . the sum of £800 on or before the 25th of that instant March and should upon reasonable notice furnish and provide such and so much good and merchantable wood and timber as sho^d be necessary for erecting and building the s^d intended houses and buildings . . . without expecting anything for such wood or Timber so that the value of the same did not exceed the sum of £250 after the rate of 35s/ by the Ton for each ton of the said timber . . . And [Bussy Mansel] should during the cont^ce of the said term on reasonable notice furnish and deliver at the s^d intended workhouses for the use of the . . . [Partners] . . . all such good clean and merchantable coals and such as were fit for copper furnaces as sho^d from time to time be requisite and reqd directly from such pit or pits as the foreman or refiner to be employed . . . should chuse and approve of without being picked or culled of the Big Coal but as it sho^d be raised throughout at the rate of 21s/ for each *weigh* . . .

. . . Covenant by the said [*Partners*] . . . that they would not during the said term buy or make use of any coals in the said intended workhouses Mills or other the premises aforesaid other than the said coals of the said B. Mansel his heirs and assigns . . .

. . . That the said . . . [*Partners*] . . . sho^d at all times during the said term oblige all such Masters or owners of Ships and

Vessels that should at any time bring any oar or other materials to the said works to load all such Coals as they should ship or take into such vessels during such respective voyages at the said Coal place or Bank called White Rock aforesaid at the usual rates or allowances . . .'

(Agreement for the establishment of the White Rock Copper Works near Swansea, 1736. Glamorgan Archive Service, D/D,XHR31.)

C.12a . . . The situation of Merthyr is picturesque . . . There are several Iron works establish'd here of considerable magnitude but those of Mr Crawshay are of the greatest extent. The expenses for labour only in his works are 3000£ a Month. The average earnings of Men Women & Children are 3£ a Month. The wages of some amount to as much as 9 Guineas pr. Month. Mr C is supposed to be clearing to the amount of *36,000[?]£ pr. annum. Indeed this sum large as it is does not seem at all improbable when you see the immensity of his works & consider at how slight an expense all the materials required for the formation of Iron are procured. Close to the spot, in the mountains above, are inexhaustible sources of Iron ore, Coal, Lime Stone, Fire [?] Stone & Fire Clay . . .

(Revd George Capper, 'Journal of a Tour in Wales', 1802. National Library of Wales MS 21235B.)

C.12b . . . Mr Crawshay's iron works of Cyfarthfa are now by far the largest in this kingdom; probably, indeed, the largest in Europe; and in that case, as far as we know, the largest in the world. He employs constantly fifteen hundred men, at an average of thirty shillings a week per man . . . Mr Crawshay now works six furnaces and two rolling mills . . . The number of smelting furnaces at Merthyr Tydvil is about sixteen.

(B.H. Malkin, *The Scenery, Antiquities and Biography of South Wales*, 1807, Vol.I, pp.266–7, based on visits in 1803.)

C.13 Two miles from Wrexham is Bersham iron furnace belonging to Messrs J. and W. Wilkinson . . . it fell to Mr John Wilkinson to prosecute renewed plans in which he succeeded wonderfully. The mechanism employed is exceedingly ingenious, and his works may be ranked among the first in the kingdom. Besides the smelting furnaces, there are several air-furnaces for re-melting the pig iron, and casting it into cylinders, water pipes, boilers, pots, pans of all sizes, cannon and ball, etc. The cannon are cast solid and bored like a wooden pipe. There are also forges for making the cast-iron malleable, and a newly erected foundry . . .

(G. Nicholson, *The Cambrian Traveller's Guide*, 1813, p.13; 'written years before' according to A.N. Palmer, 'John Wilkin-son and the Old Bersham Iron Works', *Trans. Soc. Cymmrodor-ion*, 1897–8, p.35 — the excerpt being quoted on pp.35–6.)

C.14   The Iron is at first made into Bars of 10 Inches & 1/2 in length, 3 in breadth, & 2 in. thickness; after having been 3 Times heated, doubled & pass'd thro' Rollers, it is converted into 8 Plates, each 14 Inches in length, great care having been taken every Time they pass'd thro' the Rollers to seperate the Folds; the Edges are then cut smooth, & the Sheets reduc'd to the proper Size; these are successively laid in 3 different kinds of Pickle; & after has been bent in such a Manner, that a Man can take up a Dozen at a time, they are again heated; when taken out of the Furnace, they are slightly struck against the Ground, in order to beat off those Scales wch they have contracted from the Pickle being hardned in the Fire; & when cold they are again pass'd thro' the Rollers, to smooth them entirely; they are afterwards put into 2 other sorts of Pickle; & 3 Times scowered with Hemp & Bran: The Iron Plates are now fit to be put into the first Pot of Block Tin (on the surface of which is a Coat of Tallow an Inch thick to make the Tin adhere to the Iron) where they lay half an Hour; they are then carried to the last Pot, where having been only dipp'd in, they are brush'd over to make the Tin lye smooth & equal, thrown into hot Grease to take off any superfluous spots, & scower'd 3 Times more; they are then pack'd up 150 together, in Boxes, which compleats the whole of the Business.

(Tin-plate production at the Melingriffith Works near Cardiff in

1782: the name of the writer is not known. Quoted in Gordon Tucker and Peter Wakelin, 'Metallurgy in the Wye Valley and South Wales in the late eighteenth century', *Journal of the Historical Metallurgical Society*, Vol.XV, 2, 1981, pp.98–9.)

C.15 Yours I rec.d and am glad to find that you are come to Coal . . . it will be highly [in] our Interest I shou'd think, to employ as many men as you judge proper for the workg and raising the same in Order to send to the difft. Parts of the Country you mention . . . & as the Spring I am informed is the time that the Lime Hills [*sic*] take off the small Coal, it will be for Morg.n Lloyd of Lansevin here yesterday, when we fully talked over the affair of the Coal in your Letter who heartily rejoices at the same being found, being nearer to him Llandilo and Landovery than any other works he thinks . . . I shall be glad to hear the differt Pieces of Coal and *Culme* at all the sev.l Works of Roger and where the other Labourers are — with a Plan of a regular Colliery which you mention & whether it will not be more for our Interest at first, to sell Cheaper than Others do, to induce them to come to us, and take off the Coal & *Culm* as soon as landed . . . I find in some of my Fathers Acco.ts when the Coal Works were wraught under the five adjoining farms I have near Colsbrook that the Colliers Pick Ax men and Cutters sometimes worked by the Day, but by the Pick Ax and Drays, & so paid for what Quantity of Coal & *Culme* they landed, for I find in General the Observation is, that all Colliers have been looked upon to be great Rogues & require good looking after to see that the Streets are regularly Carryed on, the Coal Work clean & Sufficient, strong Pillars, always left to support the work . . . you will [?] an honest Man for a winder to take an exact acc.t of all Coal & *Culme* Landed fairly & justly to set down the acco.t every day . . .

(John Vaughan, Golden Grove Estate, Carmarthenshire, to 'Thomas' [John Thomas, agent], undated but the year appears to be 1758. Carmarthenshire Record Office, Cawdor Vaughan Papers 102/8029; thanks are given to Mr John Owen, County Archivist, for his comment. See Major Francis Jones, 'The Vaughans of Golden Grove III', *Trans. Soc. Cymmrodorion*, 1964, Part II, p.207.)

C.16   Higher up are the Iron Mines & Collieries — one of the latter I saw. Instead of deep shafts, they are here worked by Levels driven horizontally into the sides of the Mountains, in which the workmen pursue their labours, branching off into streets as the course of the vein directs them, leaving pillars of coal at certain distances to support the roof . . . The vein of coal is not always regularly continued in the same place, but instead thereof, the Miners frequently meet with hard rock, which interrupts their further progress . . . If it be cast down, they sink a pit to it — but if it be cast up, to any considerable height, they are often obliged with great labor & expence, to carry forwards a Level, or long Gallery through the rock, till they again arrive at the stratum of Coal.

It sometimes happens that the Mines are set on fire by fulminating damps, when they produce dreadful explosions, & are very dangerous to the Miners — as was the case in a pit not far from the place which I am describing . . .

. . . The common price paid to Colliers for cutting Coal in these pits is about 2*s* 4*d* per ton long *weighs*. The proprietors sell it upon the bank at the pits mouth, at 6 shillings per Ton — Carriage from the banks to the Wharfs in Rail Waggons, from 3*s* 4*d* to 3*s* 6*d* per load, each waggon carrying about 2 Tons, 6 hundredweight — Tonnage paid for travelling on the Rail Road, 2 pence per ton per Mile. It is sold to the public at Glangrwny Wharf, at 9 Shilling per Ton short weight — & at Brecknock at 15*s* per ton Do.

(A.M. Cuyler, 'Recollections of a visit to Llanbedr' [Clydach Gorge, near Abergavenny], 1807. National Library of Wales MS 784A.)

C.17   The slate quarry is situated at the entrance of the great chasm called Nant Tranco [*sic* — for Nant Ffrancon] . . . The excavation is not very extensive or deep but tremendous enough. The number of workmen employed in the slate business may amount, on an average, to three hundred persons and Lord Penrhyn, who is the public spirited proprietor, has caused to be

The White Rock Copper and Brass Works, near Swansea, in 1744.

built a multitude of neat slated cottages, for the labourers, in the
valley and along the sides of the Ogwen . . .

(A description of the Penrhyn Slate Quarry, attributed to the
Revd Nicholas Owen, *Caernarvonshire, A Sketch of its History,
Antiquities, Mountains and Productions,* 1792, pp.33–4.)

Debating the Evidence

R.O. Roberts has chosen a set of extracts which illustrate many aspects
of the industrial history of Wales in the eighteenth century. The
evidence presented here comes mainly from two kinds of source: (1)
descriptive accounts written by observers or visitors, and (2) letters or
other documents written by men actively involved in industrial
enterprises of various kinds. In the case of the former it would be very
rash to accept everything that a casual visitor writes; with the latter one
is much closer to the real stuff of economic history — but even these
extracts need careful handling if their real significance is to be
appreciated.

Source C.1
Lewis Morris was (among other things) a surveyor; he had recently come
to live at Aberystwyth and was beginning to interest himself in lead-
mining, an important industry in the hinterland of that town. Contrast
the attitude to industrial development of the writer of the letter with
what he writes of 'John, Ben Clyttwr', who was presumably a local
farmer.

Source C.2
The writer, better known as *Iolo Morganwg*, was a Welsh-speaking
Glamorgan man, a literary scholar, antiquary and radical who is referred
to in this book in several other contexts. He was also a man with a lively
interest in contemporary industrial developments. Is this extract an
authoritative source for the history of lead-mining in Llanfyrnach?

Source C.3
For what reasons should we treat the evidence of tourists with caution?
Sir Richard Colt Hoare (1758-1838) was a Wiltshire landowner and a
distinguished antiquary, here describing what must have been one of the
first of his many tours in Wales.

Sources C.4a–C.4c

Gabriel Powell of Swansea was the powerful local agent of the Duke of Beaufort, the lord of Gower; as such, his great object was the protection and promotion of his lord's interests. There was an on-going dispute over the Duke's claim (asserted by Powell in his 'Survey' of 1764) to own the coal under the vast common lands of the lordship which had long been subject to encroachment by neighbouring gentry and *freeholders*. In what way are the statements in these extracts biased; do they represent the actual situation, or the situation Beaufort and Powell wished to exist? Also, on the basis of these extracts, would it be true to say that the Duke and his agent were prepared to allow people to dig coal as long as that coal was too inaccessible to be of any commercial value? (See Source C.16 for further information on the cost of transport of coal.)

Source C.5

Are all the statements in this document necessarily literally true? In answering it is important to think about what purpose may have lain behind the writing of these 'comments'.

Source C.6

Even though the Golden Grove estate was the largest in Carmarthenshire, with a revenue of over £3,000 per annum, the owner was looking for ways of increasing his income. In this instance the object of the sale of timber (an important part of the economy of many Welsh estates) was to reduce the burden of debt with which the Golden Grove estate had been saddled by the Duke of Bolton, a previous owner. How would you rate the reliability as an historical source of a private letter written by a man to his son?

Source C.7

Attempt an assessment of the kind of skill that Guest was looking for. What points mentioned in this extract from a letter suggest that such men were rare? Note especially Guest's nation-wide contacts (Hawkins was an ironmaster near Manchester).

Source C.8

This is a report published in a magazine and it is doubtless generally correct, though we are given no clues to judge the accuracy of the detail, such as it is.

Source C.9

Comment on the results of the exploitation of lead in the remote northern district of Carmarthenshire (Rhandir-mwyn). The mines are alleged to have brought the Campbells (Lords Cawdor) £300,000 by the end of the century. In assessing the historical value of this document would it be useful to know something of the writer's background?

Source C.10

Skinner was a Somerset parson touring Wales in 1802. He gives a vivid personal impression of his visit to the Parys copper mine, near Amlwch. As an eye-witness account written by an intelligent and well-educated man, this is a source of considerable interest and value. But is there any theoretical reason to doubt what he says? He was a casual visitor who may never have seen anything like Parys before — did he necessarily understand everything he saw?

Source C.11

As a legal document this must contain precise information, and as a lease of land for a specified period of years it is as straightforward as any deed can be — other kinds of deeds (especially those which permanently transfer the ownership of real property) can be very complicated and obscure. Summarize the content of this lease, indicating who is the lessor and who the lessees and listing the conditions which the lessees have undertaken to comply with.

Sources C.12a and C.12b

These two interesting accounts of the great Cyfarthfa ironworks at Merthyr Tydfil were written by visitors in 1802 and 1803. They provide a very salutary illustration of the danger of accepting 'facts' from such sources. You will see what I mean if you try to make sense of the information which each gives about Richard Crawshay's wage bill.

Source C.13

This description of the important ironworks of the Wilkinson Brothers at Bersham in Denbighshire probably dates from the 1790s or earlier, even though it was published in 1813. The Bersham works were especially famous for the manufacture of cannon and of cylinders for Boulton and Watt steam engines.

Source C.14

This is an apparently well-informed description of tin-plate production at Melingriffith, near Cardiff. How does the anonymity of the document affect the historian's assessment of its reliability?

Source C.15

This interesting letter from John Vaughan of Golden Grove (see also Source C.6) to his agent is mainly concerned with plans for exploiting coal newly discovered on his estate in Carmarthenshire. Considering that the substance of the letter is based partly on the writer's own knowledge and partly on hearsay, what actual facts about methods of coal-mining in the eighteenth century does it give?

Source C.16

Compare the price of a ton of coal at the pit head with the cost per ton at Brecon. Indicate how the coal was transported from the pit to the town.

Source C.17

Nicholas Owen (1752–1811) was a clergyman and antiquary who lived in Bangor, only a few miles from the slate quarry described in this extract. Should this make his evidence more reliable than that of a mere tourist? What may he have meant by describing Lord Penrhyn as 'public spirited'?

Discussion

All the documents that R.O. Roberts provides are primary sources in the sense that each was written in the eighteenth century (or in the first few years of the nineteenth) and purports to tell us about some contemporary economic activity. As suggested in the first paragraph of Debating the Evidence, however, the documents fall into two very distinct categories. The following can be called, for want of a better term, 'descriptive': Sources C.2, C.3, C.8, C.9, C.10, C.12, C.13, C.16 and C.17. They are all, in fact, essentially topographical, many of them being extracts from journals kept by tourists. By the late eighteenth century, Wales was a fashionably romantic and picturesque country much frequented by wealthy Englishmen in search of diversion. (See the chapter on 'Mythology and Tradition' for further information on this.)

It would not be wise for a historian to accept any statement from such a source without careful consideration and, where possible, cross-checking with other evidence. It could well be that the tourist had been misinformed, or he might have misunderstood what he saw or was told, since his personal knowledge of the place would have been only slight. Indeed, what he writes may reflect no more than his own fanciful perception of the scene he describes. (A notable instance of this is provided by a visitor to Flat Holm in the Bristol Channel; he saw there a heap of coal — brought in for the lighthouse — and concluded that there was a colliery on the island.) Clearly, some tourists were more knowledgeable and intelligent than others. The historian will want to make some inquiries about each writer — at the very least he will want to consult the *Dictionary of National Biography* and the *Dictionary of Welsh Biography* for basic facts. From such obvious reference books as these it becomes apparent that Edward Williams (Source C.2), B.H. Malkin (Source C.12) and Nicholas Owen (Source C.17) were far from being strangers to Wales, and so what they wrote may on that account have some authority. How much authority would have to be determined in each individual case.

The second category includes private letters and other documents written by men actively engaged in, or with direct knowledge of, industrial enterprises (Sources C.1, C.4, C.5, C.6, C.7, C.11, C.14 and C.15). Here again some research is necessary to establish the credentials of each author; in these cases it quickly becomes apparent that they knew what they were writing about. But (and it is a big 'but') interpretation is still vital and the intention of the writer is very important. This is most obviously the case with Source C.5. Although no one would doubt the fact that slate is heavy and expensive to transport, one may wonder why the Dinorwig partners were stressing this point so strongly — and to whom were their comments addressed? We are not told.

The main point to grasp is that primary sources are not *ipso facto* 'true'. There is in fact an infinite variety of primary sources and their value to the historian depends very much on who wrote them and for what purpose.

RHI. I.

CYLCH-GRAWN

CYNMRAEG;

NEU

DRYSORFA GWYBODAETH.

Rhifyn Cyntaf, Pris Chwe cheiniog.

Am CHWEFROR 1793.

Yn cynwys y pethau canlynol.

Y GWIR YN ERBYN Y BYD.

Na ymddiried i'th fyw, ond i Dduw a'i ddifgyblion.

TALIESYN.

TREFECCA:

Argraphwyd yn y Flwyddyn 1793.

Beginnings of Radicalism

GWYN A. WILLIAMS

'Dyma ni yn awr ar daith ein gobaith!' ('Here we are now on the journey of our hope!') Morgan John Rhys, a broad-minded *Baptist* who became a Jacobin (a slang term for democrat), launched his summons to the Welsh to create a free, representative and liberal new order in his *Cylchgrawn Cymraeg (Welsh*
D.3   *Journal)* of 1793 (D.3), the first Welsh-language journal seriously to discuss political issues. He put the words into the mouth of the legendary Prince *Madoc* who was believed to have discovered America in 1170 and to have left there a tribe of Welsh Indians. By the 1790s, in America, those Welsh Indians had been 'identified' as the Mandan Indians of the largely
D.1   unexplored Missouri (D.1).[1]

The American dimension is central to the history of the first Welsh radicalism. Despite its '*French Revolution*' tone, British Jacobinism generally, with Tom Paine as its symbol, was essentially an Anglo-American movement. Welsh radicalism was the most American component of it.

Welsh-American *Dissenters* were over-represented in America and prominent in its Revolution; they remained in direct and close contact with Welsh *Dissenters* at home, who took the lead in political reform movements which responded strongly in turn to the challenge of the *French Revolution*. Moreover, during the crisis years of 1795–6 and 1800–1, there was a significant emigration from Wales, which sent
D.12   thousands to America (D.12) (with penniless thousands more clamouring to get away) and sent many of them over charged with the idea of regaining contact with the Lost Brethren, the
D.2   Welsh Indians, to create a Free Wales in the West (D.2, D.6,
D.6   D.7, D.8).

D.7   In America, radicals like Morgan John Rhys, freed from
D.8   inhibition, could voice opinions only hinted at in Wales
D.6   (D.6). In the abundant private correspondence which survives, every single Welshman who wrote to a spiritual brother in the new USA called himself, in the most revolutionary French style, a '*Sans-culotte* Republican' (Pennepek). When Welsh people applied for American citizenship in the USA, the majority described their homeland (illegally, indeed treasonably) as the Kingdom of Wales.

Their Jacobinism, like that of the London-Welsh intellectuals, was the vehicle for a romantic and radical nationalism. And the American example, charged now with French styles, drenched every radical and protest movement in the turbulent Wales of the 1790s — in books, leaflets, journals and graffiti, in the chanted slogans of Machynlleth pubs and Bala rioters, in the speeches at nocturnal mass meetings in Llanbrynmair or a Denbigh in the grip of armed and organized crowds and in the Address published in insurrectionary Merthyr Tydfil in 1801, which prefigures the next forty years on

D.5   the southern coalfield (D.5, D.9, D.13). This American dimen-
D.9   sion has been rediscovered but recently, like a lost Atlantis. It
D.13   locates Welsh Jacobinism in a wider and deeper context.

A RECEIVED WISDOM AND ITS INADEQUACIES

An American provenance for the first Welsh radicalism is certainly recognized in the 'received wisdom' on this subject.[2]

This interpretation accepts that 'politics' in Wales begins with the American Revolution, perceived by many as a British civil war and by Welsh *Dissenters*, subjected to legal discrimination, as a challenge to win full citizenship. It notes that Welsh book production accelerates from the 1770s; the number of political texts multiplies six-fold. Out of this, Britain's first post-colonial crisis, grow the reform movements associated with *John Wilkes*, the County Association movement of Christopher Wyvill and the Society for Constitutional Information with its full democratic programme.

These movements had some impact on Wales: for example,

the 1782 trial for seditious libel of the Dean of St Asaph, who had published a pamphlet against the American War by his brother-in-law, the Orientalist Sir William Jones. His acquittal evoked a major popular rally in the Wrexham-Ruabon area, which was later to be disturbed by the pro-French propaganda of the Jacobin industrialists John Wilkinson and Josiah Wedgwood and was to become the theatre of an organized popular rebellion in the 1790s. The *Wilkes* affair touched Glamorgan and Pembrokeshire; a scatter of radicals, liberal *Dissenters* and bohemian intellectuals committed to a Welsh revival emerged; in the 1780s, the radicalized London-Welsh society of the *Gwyneddigion* took the lead.

Out of a Glamorgan in the throes of modernization, came two major, international philosophers of the age of Atlantic Revolution. *Dr Richard Price*, a prolific *Unitarian* thinker who supported the Americans, was invited to serve as financial adviser to the new USA, preached a sermon which provoked *Edmund Burke* into writing his classic of conservatism, and died in 1791, to send the new French National Assembly into official mourning for him. The younger *David Williams* became a *Deist*, wrote in defence of the Americans, was made a Citizen of the new French Republic, crossed to France to advise on its democratic constitution and devised a *Deist* liturgy which informed the National Religion of that republic.

Such people plunged into the turmoil of the 1790s — war against France, government repression, successive waves of anti-Jacobin witch-hunts, forced industrialization and agrarian modernization, social crises and an accelerating advance of *Methodism* and 'methodized' *Dissent*. In its examination of the role of Jacobinism within this cauldron of competing ideologies, the 'conventional wisdom' treats it solely as an intellectual phenomenon and treats it at three levels.

Richard Price and *David Williams* are considered to be people who wrote in England and in English for a wider world and their influence on Wales is assumed to be negligible. Then there were Welshmen outside Wales who addressed themselves to their compatriots. Foremost were the passionate antiquarians, scholars and preachers of national revival, the London-Welsh *Gwyneddigion*, in alliance with *Iolo Morganwg*.

SEREN TAN GWMMWL,

NEU

YCHYDIG SYLW

AR

FRENHINOEDD, ESCOBION, ARGLWYDDI, &c.

A

LLYWODRAETH LLOEGR

YN GYFFREDIN.

Wedi ei ysgrifennu er mwyn y Cymru uniaith.

GAN

JOHN JONES, GLAN-Y-GORS, BARDD.

Y GWIR YN ERBYN Y BYD.

" Ar y gwir mae rhagoriaeth
" O'm lleddir am wir ba waeth."

IEUAN TEW.

LLUNDAIN:

ARGRAPHWYD, AC AR WERTH, GAN VAUGHAN GRIFFITHS
RHIF 169, STRAND.

PRIS SWLLT.

The *Gwyneddigion*, enmeshed with the London radicals around *William Blake*, published scholarly texts and radical nationalist propaganda. From 1789, in alliance with like-minded men in north Wales, they revived the *eisteddfod*, tried to make it into a national academy and an instrument of Jacobinism. Before the counter-revolution engulfed them, their prize subjects were democratic and their prize medals were struck by M. Dupré, who became official engraver to the French Republic. *Iolo Morganwg*, from 1792, offered the Welsh a dazzling, if largely mythical, vision of their own past and presented his 'rediscovered' *Gorsedd* of Bards of the Island of Britain as a democratic élite of People's Remembrancers to a nation reborn in liberty. *Jac Glan-y-gors* (John Jones),a member of this circle, published *Toriad y Dydd* (*Daybreak*) (1795) and *Seren dan Gwmwl* (*The Clouded Star*) (1797), which were the Welsh versions of the ideas of Tom Paine.[3]

The 'conventional wisdom' records the devotion of these men, but also registers their failure in face of the reaction and the apostasy of many — Iolo and Jac were to sing in praise of Nelson and the Volunteers (although Iolo's 'apostasy' was evidently mere self-protection — witness his response to the French landing at Fishguard) (D.10). It is even more dismissive of the handful of Welshmen at home who wrote in Welsh. Morgan John Rhys brought out his *Cylchgrawn* in 1793; it ran for five issues. Its successors, the *Drysorfa* (1795) of Tomos Glyn Cothi (Thomas Evans) and the *Geirgrawn* (1796) of David Davies were even more short-lived. Thomas Roberts's *Cwyn yn erbyn Gorthrymder* (*Protest against Oppression*) (1798) was the most specifically Welsh of all the Jacobin texts, but it could not stand against *Gair yn ei Amser* (*A Word in Season*) (1798), the politically quietist manifesto of the *Methodist*, *Thomas Jones*.

Welsh society, largely illiterate in English, backward and in the grip of the gentry and the clergy, proved impenetrable. The new and growing power of *Methodism* and the more con-servative elements of *Dissent* were hostile. War with France, the repression, the patriotic rally after the French landing in Fishguard in 1797, defeated the Welsh Jacobins. Recognizable 'precursors' of democracy in Wales, they were in their own time a marginal and transient phenomenon.

D.10

TORIAD Y DYDD;

NEU

SYLW BYR

AR

HEN GYFREITHIAU

AC

ARFERION LLYWODRAETHOL:

YNGHYD A

CHRYBWYLLIAD AM FREINTIAU DYN, &c.

WEDI EI YSGRIFENNU ER MWYN Y CYMRY UNIAITH.

GAN J. JONES, GLAN Y GORS,

AWDWR Y LLYFR A ELWIR "SEREN TAN GWMMWL."

Y GWIR YN ERBYN Y BYD.

" A fo'n gam, ni fyn y gwir;
" Fo'n uniawn, ni fyn anwir."

HUW ARWYSTL.

L L U N D A I N:

ARGRAPHWYD AC AR WERTH GAN YR AWDWR, A CHAN
W. BAYNES, RHIF 54, PATERNOSTER-ROW.

1797

Gwerth chwecheining.

Certainly there is a basic truth in this argument. The Jacobins were a minority and they were defeated. The thesis as it stands, however, is no longer tenable.

The assumption that internationally renowned spokesmen made no contact with monoglot Welsh at home grotesquely exaggerates their isolation. *Richard Price* went home every summer and his kinsfolk were radical colonizers of the Welsh mind. David Jones, the Welsh *Freeholder*, preached the doctrines of the *Unitarian* democrat *Dr Joseph Priestley* as a way of life; the *Unitarian* hub in Wales was 'buried' among Welsh speakers on the Teifi, in the Black Spot of the *Calvinists*. The vocabulary of such people was common discourse. By 1800, the growing industrial village of Merthyr was taking weekly consignments of journals from London.

A classic example is provided by Morgan John Rhys's *Cylchgrawn* itself. In the fourth number, he printed chapter fifteen of the celebrated *Les Ruines* of *Constantin de Volney*. Published in 1791, *Volney*'s *Ruins*, a classic of the radical French *Enlightenment*, became a standard text for democratic and working-class movements in Britain for three generations. Its key chapter appeared in Welsh four years earlier than in English.[4] For that matter, both *Goethe*'s *Werther* and a *Beaumarchais* play were 'broadcast' in Wales within a year of original publication. 'Backward' Wales was in the throes of modernization and the most advanced European ideas penetrated swiftly.

More seriously, the 'conventional wisdom' takes no cognizance of two fundamental and related phenomena, which have but recently been restored to history. Between 1795 and 1801, western Wales was a 'disturbed district', repeatedly convulsed by riot, protest and rebellion.[5] Much of that popular action was charged with the ideas of the Jacobins. Closely related to the 'disturbed district' was the migration to America from 1793 onwards.

From the 1780s, contact between the established Welsh communities in America and Wales was revivified. It is the *Baptist* connection which is particularly well documented. Dr Samuel Jones of Pennepek Chapel in Philadelphia became the focal centre of a transatlantic correspondence which embraced the *Baptist* college in Providence, Rhode Island (later Brown University). That correspondence brings to life a veritable *Baptist* International, in ideas, books, ultimately people, which even had its own ships — three or four favoured vessels run by the Loxley family of Philadelphia (into which Morgan John Rhys married). This *Baptist* correspondence (to which there was a *Congregationalist* parallel, hinted at by the surviving documents) is not only a prime source for the migration movement of the 1790s; it throws a flood of light on attitudes and actions back in Wales.[6]

Nor is there any sense in this 'conventional wisdom' that the Welsh Jacobins were not the starting-point of a long and potent tradition. There was a direct, face-to-face transmission of the democratic ideology from the 1790s to the increasingly 'working-class' radicals of the early nineteenth century. This is particularly visible in the textile districts of the Severn in mid-Wales, in the disturbed hinterland of Carmarthen and in the iron and coal valleys of the south-east.

The central weakness of the 'conventional wisdom', in short, is that it compartmentalizes. It treats as distinct issues, attitudes and actions which were in fact intimately related. It fails to integrate Welsh Jacobinism into the social reality of an eighteenth-century Wales which was an Atlantic province of a novel Great Britain.

A Society and its Intellectuals

The Union of England and Scotland in 1707 was a significant punctuation point in the process which transformed two off-shore islands of Europe into Great Britain, the seat of a world-wide commercial empire. In that process, its backward province of Wales became an export sector of an Atlantic economy.

Ninety per cent of British copper, tin-plate and related industries was concentrated around Swansea and Neath, geared to Atlantic export. The cloth trade had migrated to mid and north Wales, where a farm-based industry, under the control of the *Shrewsbury Drapers*, sent its products, both the flannels of Montgomeryshire and the rougher webs and stockings of Merioneth, to the Gulf of Mexico and other American destinations. This industry turned a great tract of 'rural' Wales, stretching from Machynlleth in a great arc through Merioneth and Montgomeryshire to the Denbighshire border country, into a network of factory-parishes dependent on outlets like the busy little Atlantic port of Barmouth. Lead, and every other mineral, was busily exploited, while the cattle export trade bred banks and a new breed of entrepreneur; there were the beginnings of another British export monopoly in slate. In the early eighteenth century, an iron industry based on scattered charcoal furnaces was already supplying a sixth of British pig iron and, from the 1760s, the opening up of the coalfields in north-east and south-east Wales heralded a major expansion.

Merchant capitalism, with its multiplying rural workers in industry, artisans, shippers, salesmen, drovers, was sending pulses of change through slow-moving parishes. Throughout the century, there was a remorseless rise in the numbers of artisans, workers in the service trades, shopkeepers, teachers, doctors, lawyers of humble origin. As these 'lower-middle orders' rose, the traditional lesser gentry of Wales, multi-tudinous in consequence of the old kindred system, lost their grip and their political status, disappeared from public life or were forced to adjust.

In the last years of the century, growth accelerated. The invention of the *puddling process* turned the southern coalfield into the prime centre of the British iron industry; forty per cent of its pig iron was produced there, in huge, integrated and mushrooming enterprises. The momentous migration into the south-east began. At this stage, the north-eastern coalfield was no less breakneck in its growth. The outbreak of war with France in 1793 — a war that was to last a generation — thrust a crisis of modernization on the rural cloth industry. New entrepreneurs from Lancashire moved in to prise loose the grip of Shrewsbury; the first factories rose on the Severn, a small class of native employers clawed their way up, as many farmer-artisans were driven into the ranks of the *proletariat*. At the same time, modernizing landowners resorted to *enclosures*, the annual lease and other innovations in the harsh context of war, with its inflation, taxes, levies of men for the militia and the navy, grain shortages and the closure of the port of Barmouth. As the coalfields boomed, traditional society in west and north Wales lurched into social crisis. The rapid growth of *Methodism* and an evangelical *Dissent* in north and west was one human response.

The all-powerful class of gentry which controlled this society was itself in the throes of change. This was most dramatic in Glamorgan, as a recent study has revealed.[7] In little more than a generation, the Glamorgan gentry were transformed; by 1750, only ten of thirty-one great estates were still in the hands of the original families; there was an infusion of new men, many of them English. They were hugely wealthy: nineteen men in Glamorgan owned more land than the seven richest nobles of Toulouse in France: forty-seven men owned eighty per cent of the county. They were modernizers, they prepared their lands for the advance of industry. From mid-century onwards, they abandoned the romantic *Jacobitism* of their forebears and embraced a *Whig* Great Britain with its 'blue-water' strategy of commercial imperialism. In the process, they tended to forget their predecessors' paternalist concern for their Welsh tenants and their Welsh culture. A spiritual vacuum opened up in Glamorgan, partly filled by a new opposition drawn from former *Tories* but attracting the newer men from the 'lower-middle orders'. The lodges of *Freemasonry* were its breeding-grounds and in the crisis of the American Revolution, that opposition went patriot in quasi-Jacobin style. These were the men who recruited *Richard Price* and *Iolo Morganwg* as their election writers, men drawn from the lively bilingual artisan culture of the Vale of Glamorgan with its links to the tougher *Dissenting* radicalism of the hill country, now going *Presbyterian-Unitarian* and to the radical and often *Unitarian* circles of London.

Glamorgan was an extreme example, but similar changes may be detected in Pembrokeshire, Monmouthshire, Anglesey and, above all, Denbighshire. Societies west of the central massif were slower to change; a growing concentration of land-ownership tended to squeeze out the lesser gentry, many of whom found compensation in the *Methodism* which offered an alternative source of local authority. The demographic crisis of the gentry in general was nothing like as severe as in Glamorgan, but a proliferation of Welsh heiresses brought intruders, many of them Anglo-Scottish, and from mid-century, as nostalgic *Jacobitism* was abandoned, the Welsh *magnates* and gentry shifted from the old politics to the new. So did the opposition. In the ten years after 1760, the number of *Freemasons'* lodges in Wales rose from six to sixteen.

An intellectual and spiritual vacuum opened in a society which was steadily being drained of any specifically Welsh identity. Into this vacuum moved *Dissent, Methodism* and romantic nationalism.

It was in the eighteenth century, through the sustained campaigns for literacy symbolized by the celebrated *circulating schools* of Griffith Jones, that the Welsh people learned to read; a majority of adults probably became technically literate in Welsh. They learned to read in terms of the Bible and of Protestant sectarianism. This was probably one source of the *Methodist* movement within the Anglican Church which grew slowly from the 1730s, passionate, evangelical, sometimes ecstatic, but also highly organized, hierarchical and authoritarian. During the last quarter of the eighteenth century, as modernization intensified, the growth of *Methodism* accelerated as it swept into the troubled west and north. The sects of the old *Dissent* were swept along with it, in a series of mass mission campaigns into the disturbed districts. In the process, many caught the evangelical fever and there was a prolonged crisis of growth within *Dissent*, as the newer styles challenged its old rationalism and radicalism.

The *Baptists* split wide open and there was turmoil among *Independents* and *Presbyterians*, as a newer religious rationalism, grounded in the *Enlightenment*, resisted the 'methodized' evangelicals. Nonconformity, officially joined by the Anglican *Methodists* after 1811, advanced so rapidly that over little more than a generation it captured a majority of the Welsh (one of the most remarkable transformations in the history of any people). But it advanced through contradiction and controversy which turned Welsh intellectual life into a cockpit of competing ideologies.

During the troubled 1790s, one curate in Anglesey wrote in anguish to the King, claiming that north Wales was being 'overrun' by 'hordes of *Methodists* descanting on the Rights of

Man'; a magistrate humiliated by armed and organized crowds in Denbigh blamed the rebellion on *Methodists*. In that time and at those places some *Methodists* may well have been social rebels, but the official leadership of *Methodism* and the more evangelical *Dissent*, and its mass propaganda, was politically quietist and even *Tory*. It was the rationalist *Dissenters* who were radical.

They found a vanguard in the *Unitarianism* which grew from a handful of chapels on the Teifi which, in the early eighteenth century, embraced *Arianism* and denied the divinity of Christ. This radical break from orthodoxy led them into ever wider fields of rationalist heresy. Thinking of this order captured the small *Presbyterian* denomination whose very title came simply to mean liberalism in theology. It made inroads into *Independence*, particularly in Glamorgan, Denbighshire and parts of Carmarthenshire. It informed the schism among the *Baptists*. A specific *Unitarian* denomination took shape in south Wales in 1802, but people of this temper were present among most denominations and a considerable number ran off the Christian spectrum altogether, to embrace *Deism*.

These were the men who took the lead in every reform campaign — against the slave trade, for the emancipation of *Dissent*, for parliamentary reform, in support of the American and *French Revolutions*. They were increasingly affected by the fashionable intellectual millenarianism of the time. Before he launched the *Cylchgrawn*, Rhys had crossed to revolutionary France to preach the Protestant liberty of prophecy's Last Days and had persuaded the *Baptist* associations of south-west Wales to finance a French translation of an old *Puritan* and unorthodox Bible.

These men found political allies among people very different in style — the bohemian intellectuals of a romantic Welsh nationalism. This movement had sprung from, indeed exploded out of, a hard, century-long labour by the Morris brothers of Anglesey, their London-Welsh Cymmrodorion Society and its allies, to rescue and revive lost Welsh traditions, to print and reprint classical poetry, history, dictionaries. Their successors in the *Gwyneddigion*, active freethinkers mostly, Owen Jones, William Owen, *Iolo Morganwg* and the like, up to their eyes in the ferment of artisan London at the climax of what seemed an

Atlantic Revolution, were swept into their own form of millenarianism.

Their radicalism, in a creative outburst which resurrected an *eisteddfod*, created a *Gorsedd of Bards*, revived *Madoc* and launched a new vision of history, expressed a nationalism as romantic as that which convulsed many of their counterparts in the little lost nations of Europe — Czechs, Slovaks, Slovenes, Catalans. *Iolo Morganwg* was Wales's version of the romantic poet who spoke for such peoples. Characteristically, Iolo made his Druids *Unitarian* and claimed that their liberal creed had been transmitted through the secret books of the *Freemasons*![8]

In the late eighteenth century, in short, the modernization of Wales generated a loose-textured but potent organic intelligentsia which preached democracy to the Welsh in millenarian terms. At first, they operated within the shelter of a 'respectable' patriot opposition which had emerged in regions like Glamorgan and Denbighshire. That protection disappeared in the panic response to the second *French Revolution* of August 1792, which overthrew and killed a king and created a democratic republic in blood and terror. All over Britain, the respectable recoiled from democracy even as thousands of artisans and the 'lower orders' flocked to join their unprecedented popular societies. Over the winter of 1792–3, the lawyer John Reeves, with covert government support, organized a massive McCarthyite campaign of 'loyalism' in an attack on the press and reformers of every stripe, with Church and King mobs baying through the streets. The campaign climaxed in the declaration of war against France in February 1793. The Welsh radicals were hit as hard as any others; the *Gorsedd* was treated as a subversive organization. Morgan John Rhys, with *Gwyneddigion* support, brought out the *Cylchgrawn* to butt its way against the storm, but in 1794 came the second spasm of repression, witch-hunts, the opening of mail, mass arrests, more street mobs and the *Treason Trials* (D.4).

D.4

Jacobinism was driven underground. It dwindled into private correspondence, itself unsafe from government spies (much of the 'apostasy' of Jacobins can be explained in such terms). It was precisely at that point, however, that Welsh Jacobins, like their colleagues in England, were offered access to a wider audience in the wave of troubles which broke in 1795.

VOTING WITH THEIR FEET

Central to the troubles of 1795–6 and 1800–1 were grain shortages and famine prices, to which crowds all over Britain responded in a classic reaffirmation of the 'moral economy' of the fair price and the just wage; they took over markets and fixed prices, they stopped the export of local foodstuffs, they clashed with soldiers. So serious was the movement that in 1795, with the war effort paralysed, Pitt asked the French for peace terms. In 1800–1, it was even worse, since Jacobins and trade unionists emerged from the shadows and real insurrection threatened (it was partly to materialize in the nation-wide insurrection plans associated with the *Despard conspiracy*). Britain was driven to the *Peace of Amiens.*

In Wales, forced recruitment for the militia and the navy were additional grievances and behind it all to west and north was the crisis in the cloth trade and the advance of capitalist farming in a traditional community.[9] In 1795 price riots and crowd actions broke out all over Wales — Bangor, Conwy, Aberystwyth, Narberth, Bridgend; huge gangs of colliers scoured the north-eastern coalfield; hundreds of men in military formation seized Denbigh, imprisoned the magistrates and forced them to sign a 'treaty', while a small farmer, John Jones, made speeches evoking the arguments over representation and taxation of the American crisis (D.5). There were riots in the south-west and, at Haverfordwest (a notorious Jacobin stronghold), a virtual insurrection. Over the winter of 1796–7, resistance to conscription plunged Merioneth and Montgomeryshire into turmoil. There were large-scale riots against the militia and the *Navy Act*; Bala, Barmouth and Machynlleth were storm-centres. Mass meetings for months on end, around the troubled cloth centre of Llanbrynmair, demanded a government of the poor not the rich (D.9). Soldiers were repeatedly marching and counter-marching through little Bala and there were Jacobin toasts in its pubs.

Hardly had the country settled, when the French staged their

D.5

D.9

This day was publifhed,

AN

ADDRESS to the PEOPLE

OF THE UNITED KINGDOM OF

Great Britain and Ireland,

ON THE THREATENED

INVASION.

EXTRACTS FROM THE ABOVE WORK.

AMONG the inexpreffibly dreadful confequences which are fure to attend the conqueft of your Ifland by the French, there is one of fo horrible a nature, as to deferve diftinct notice. This barbarous, but moft artful people, when firft they invade a country in the conqueft of which they apprehend any difficulty, in order to obtain the confidence of the people, compel their troops to obferve the ftricteft difcipline, and often put a foldier to death for ftealing the moft trifling article. Like fpiders they artfully weave a web round their victim, before they begin to prey upon it. But when their fuccefs is complete they then let loofe their troops, with refiftlefs fury, to commit the moft horrible exceffes, and to pillage, burn, and defolate, without mercy, and without diftinction. But the practice to which I particularly allude will make your blood freeze in your veins. Thefe wretches are accuftomed, whenever they prevail, to fubject the women to the moft brutal violence, which they perpetrate with an infulting ferocity, of which the wildeft favages would be incapable. To gratify their furious paffions is not however their chief object in thefe atrocities. Their principal delight is to fhock the feelings of fathers and brothers, and hufbands ! Will you, my Countrymen, while you can draw a trigger, or handle a pike, fuffer your daughters, your fifters, and wives, to fall into the power of fuch monfters ?

Specimens of French Ferocity and Brutality in Wales.

It is well known that in the laft War fome French troops fucceeded in effecting a landing in Wales. They were greatly fuperior to the regular force which happened to be in the part of the country where they landed : but, upon feeing, at a diftance, a number of Welch women with red cloaks, whom they miftook for foldiers, they furrendered ! The following proofs of their ferocity and brutality are well attefted.

A peafant whom they had compelled to affift them in landing their ftores, prefumed to afk for fome compenfation, upon which the commanding Officer drew a piftol, and SHOT THE POOR FELLOW THROUGH THE HEART.

Two Officers went to a houfe, in which was a woman in child-bed, attended by her mother, who was upwards of Seventy Years old. The French brutes tied the hufband with cords, and, in his prefence, defiled both the wife and the mother ! ! !

LONDON

Printed by H. Bryer, Bridewell Hofpital, Bridge Street.

The Address is sold by J. DOWNES, Temple Bar ; J. SPRAGG, King Street Covent Garden ; J. ASPERNE, Cornhill ; and J. HATCHARD, Piccadilly.

Price Two-pence each, or Twelve Shillings the Hundred, and Eighteen-pence per Dozen.

A memento of Fishguard in 1797.

comic-opera landing in Fishguard, to provoke a patriotic spasm
and a witch-hunt against *Dissenters*. The patriotism did not last
beyond 1798. In 1800, it was officially reported that the working
people of the north-eastern coalfield were totally disaffected;
pikes were being manufactured and the government seriously
feared an armed insurrection throughout north Wales. On the
southern coalfield, and for the first time, insurrection gripped
D.13   Merthyr Tydfil and gripped it for eighteen months (D.13). Only
the peace with France brought respite.

These revolts are, of course, significant in themselves. While
not 'political' in the sense of being the product of an organized
movement, they were violent expressions of a *malaise* which
could not help being political. They cannot be dismissed as
'non-political'.[10] Moreover, these actions were steeped in the
language of the Jacobins, whether it was the speeches of John
Jones in Denbigh or of a Republican small farmer in Anglesey
D.11   (D.11) or the actions of the crowd who forced a magistrate to
wear wooden clogs to experience what the French had rebelled
D.5   against (D.5). The great storms left behind a residue of radicals
all over Wales, concentrated in particular on the textile centres
of the Severn, the troubled hinterland of Carmarthen and the
coalfields. The Address issued by rebels in Merthyr in 1801
D.13   constituted a veritable political programme (D.13).

One feature is striking. The core of continuous disturbance
was the cloth district of mid and north Wales. This was precisely
a heartland of the migration movement. The rioters of
Llanbrynmair were friends and kinsfolk of people who had just
left for the Land of the Free. A key figure was *William Jones*, a
vinegary *Voltairean* from the cloth village of Llangadfan, a
Welsh revivalist in touch with the Londoners. He never left his
parish for more than a fortnight but was better informed on
America than His Majesty's Ministers. He it was who, at the
Llanrwst *Eisteddfod* of 1791, had circulated an Address hailing
D.1   the 'discovery' of the Welsh Indians on the Missouri (D.1).

The *Madoc* myth is central to the migration and to Welsh
Jacobinism in general. The discovery of the Mandan Indians on
the Missouri (who at once became the target of the rival fur-
trade imperialisms of Britain, Spain and the USA) set off a
Madoc fever in America which was transmitted to Wales

through the publication of a learned study by a London-Welsh clergyman in 1791. The response was electric among Welsh radicals and *Dissenters* now struggling against the odds. *Iolo Morganwg* not only read a paper on the Welsh Indians to the Royal Society; he prepared a plan for a Welsh liberty settlement in the west alongside the Lost Brothers — a project which haunted the whole migration movement (D.2).

D.2

John Evans of Waunfawr near Caernarfon threw up home and job, moved to a colony of Welsh Jacobins in London, crossed to Baltimore in the steerage and started walking into the wilderness of Spanish territory beyond St Louis. After a first abortive attempt to go up the unexplored Missouri alone, he finally enrolled in the Missouri Company, Spain's last imperial venture in North America and, in Spanish service, became the first white man to reach the Mandans from St Louis. He held them against the Canadian companies for Spain and ultimately for the USA, only to die at 29 in New Orleans in drink and disillusion.[11]

And after him in 1794, went Morgan John Rhys, giving up the struggle at home, to go on a horseback tour of the American Republic, to fight for a black church in Georgia and for Indian rights on the Missouri, finally to launch the *gwladfa*, a national home for the Welsh, in Beulah, Pennsylvania. And after both of them from 1793 went hundreds of Welsh families, making their way through riots, redcoats, Algerian corsairs and hideous crossings which cost half the lives on board, to reach their new Free Wales in the West, while behind them, thousands trapped in poverty clamoured to escape. From the cloth country of mid and north Wales they came, and from the south-west, politically quiet, but slithering into its own occult *malaise* which was to debouch into the *Rebecca Riots*.[12]

Their Free Wales in Beulah failed, broken by the opening of easier Ohio lands and the abrupt acceleration of Welsh emigration around 1800. The Welsh dispersed into an anonymous America. Their fellows back home were defeated. When war was resumed, it was in different circumstances and against the tyrant Napoleon. The Jacobins vanished into the underground; many of their spokesmen were driven out of the historical memory of the Welsh.

TRADITION

Yet, in that underground, they established a new political tradition in Wales. The addresses and pamphlets which came D.13 out in Merthyr (D.13) during the insurrection of 1800–1 (when two miners were hanged) not only set out a political programme; they indicate a connection with nation-wide insurrectionary plans linked to the *Despard conspiracy*. This is the spiritual climate of the *Chartist march on Newport* forty years later. It fixes the style of those forty years.

The Jacobin tradition was transmitted, face-to-face, through the *Unitarians* and other dissidents to the new Wales. Throughout the early nineteenth century a kind of 'radical triangle' repeatedly reappears in Wales, linking the textile townships on the Severn, the hinterland of Carmarthen and the iron and coal settlements on the southern coalfield. These had been precisely the regions where Jacobinism had won some popular following. *Volney*'s *Ruins* had been printed by Morgan John Rhys in 1793; it was reprinted, word for word from his journal, in *Udgorn Cymru*, the *Chartist* newspaper of the 1840s.

This can serve as a symbol for a historic truth. Jacobinism in Wales, defeated in its own time, created a new political tradition in Wales whose ultimate expression was Welsh *Chartism*.

This can serve as a symbol for a historic truth. Jacobinism in Wales, defeated in its own time, created a new political tradition in Wales whose ultimate expression was Welsh *Chartism*.

Notes

1. G.A. Williams, *Madoc*, 1987.
2. David Williams, *A History of Modern Wales*, 1977, and *Welsh History Review*, 1967, on his work.
3. Prys Morgan, *The Eighteenth-Century Renaissance*, 1981; G.A. Williams, 'Romanticism in Wales', in *Romanticism in a National Context*, 1988.
4. G.A. Williams, 'Morgan John Rhys and Volney's *Ruins*', *Bulletin of the Board of Celtic Studies*, xx, 1962.
5. D.J.V. Jones, *Before Rebecca*, 1973.
6. G.A. Williams, *Madoc*, and *The Search for Beulah Land*, 1980.
7. Philip Jenkins, *The Making of a Ruling Class: The Glamorgan Gentry 1640–1790*, 1983.
8. Morgan, *Renaissance*; Williams, *Romanticism*.
9. Jones, *Before Rebecca*.

10 E.J. Hobsbawm, *Primitive Rebels*, 1971; G.A. Williams, 'The Primitive
Rebel and the history of the Welsh', in *The Welsh in their History*, 1982.
11 Williams, *Madoc*.
12 Williams, *Beulah Land*.

Sources

D.1   To All Indigenous Cambro-Britons: Permit me at this juncture
to congratulate you on the agreeable intelligence lately received
from America, viz, that the colony which Madog ab Owain
Gwynedd carried over the Atlantic in the twelfth century are at
this time a free and distinct people, and have preserved their
liberty, language and some traces of their religion to this very
day . . . our countrymen have not bent the knee to Baal, nor
sold their birthright for a mess of pottage, they are at this time a
free people . . .

(6–7 August 1791. Copy of an address circulated at the Llanrwst
Eisteddfod by William Jones, Llangadfan, and enclosed in a
letter to William Owen Pughe. National Library of Wales MS
13221, fo.339–43.)

D.2   1. To petition Congress for their interfering assistance in
purchasing, on peaceful and equitable terms, of the Indians, a
portion of land near the Mississippi between the Ohio and the
Illinois.

2. As soon as 100 Welsh emigrants exclusive of Women and
Children are obtained, to engage a vessel to carry them over.

3. As there are none rich, it is requisite that each person or
family should be able to pay the proper quota towards defraying
the expense of passage and land travelling.

4. Those who are able to purchase land, to give freely for ever
as many acres as necessary for raising provisions for their
families or otherwise to require no other payment than X
months' labour for every acre to the donor.

5. That Plans of Government and Religious Polity on the
purest principles of Justice, Peace and Liberty shall be assented
to by solemn affirmation and manual signature by every
emigrant before he can be admitted of the party.

Edward Williams (Iolo Morganwg). (*Source: National Library of Wales.*)

6. That such mechanics as appear to be remarkably skilful and of good character shall with consent of the majority be taken over at the expense of the Association provided such mechanics shall engage to follow their profession for seven days.

7. The mechanics deemed necessary and to be taken over at the common expense are Masons, Carpenters, Smiths, Miners, Weavers, Fullers, Potters, Braziers etc., schoolmasters.

8. Every one that can pay £5 towards the Land-Purchase money, exclusive of passage and travelling expenses, to be admitted of another company of Mechanics, who are to be endowed with proper privileges during the time they shall follow their several occupations.

9. That none be admitted of the Company who cannot speak Welsh or have at least a wife that can.

10. That the legal language of the Colony shall be Welsh and all pleadings in Law, all religious worship etc. shall be in it, the English also to be taught as a learned language and source of knowledge.

11. To purchase a common Library, 2 copies of Chambers' Cyclopedia, 1 of the Scotch Cyclopedia, Pryde's Mineralogy, Watson's Chemistry, 5 copies Owen's Dictionary, for a Select Society.

required of Congress
1. some pieces of cannon
2. a garrison to be paid by the Colonists.

('Plan of a Welsh Colony', April 1792, by Iolo Morganwg, to be submitted to the American Minister. Note the choice of 'affirmation' rather than 'oath'. National Library of Wales MS 13104, fo.28–62.)

D.3   Newyddion Pellenig a Chartrefol
... Yn yr *eisteddfod* ddiwethaf yn nhre' Derby, dygwyd dau ddyn ger bron y llys am werthu gwaith Mr Paine ar Ddynol Hawl (*The Rights of Man*). Mynnodd y rheithwyr (jury) ddarllain y llyfr a chwedi ei ystyried yn fanol, barnasant nad oedd y gwerthwyr yn euog — Not guilty.
Dygwyd gwr yn Llundain (Mr Wood) o flaen y llys, am argraphu annerchiad Paine at yr annerchwyr:- cafodd y

rheithwyr eu hanfon gan arglwydd Kenyon ddwy waith i ystyried yr achos, a chwedi aros yn hir bob tro, barnasant fod y dyn yn euog o argraphu'r llyfr, eithr nad oedd yn euog o un gosp. Er bod rhai'n cael myned yn rhydd, y mae llawer yn cael eu carcharu am argraphu a gwerthu gwaith y gwr uchod.

. . . Dywedir fod y rhyfel presennol yn sefyll i'r ddeyrnas hon mewn pymtheg can o bynnau bob awr . . . Dyma'r fendith i ryfel!

. . . Y maent wedi cyhoeddi yn senedd Paris fod Pitt yn elyn dynolryw.

. . . Y mae Marat, un o aelodau'r senedd-dy (Convention) yn Paris wedi ei ladd gan Sharlotte Corde . . . Yr oedd y Marat hwn, mae'n debyg, yn un o'r Jacobins mwyaf yn Paris ac, o bossibl, yn dymuno'n dda i'r wlad . . .

. . . Yn awr yw'r pryd i'r byddinoedd cyssylltiedig i wneud eu goreu i ddifetha Ffraingc; canys as gall y Ffrangcod ond dala ychydig o fisoedd yn fwy, o bossibl yr unant au'u gilydd, ac yna fe fydd mor anhawdd eu gorchfygu ag attal y haul yn godi . . . Y mae'r llythr a gafwyd yn Ffraingc oddiwrth Pitt wedi cynhyrfu senedd Paris yn anghyffredin; y maent yn dywedyd fod llywodraeth Lloegr yn ymddwyn yn deilwng o fwrddwyr tu ag attynt; trwy hirio cynnifer o ddynion yn ddirgelaidd i yrru'r wlad ben-ben ac i ladd eu gilydd. Os ydyw'r hanes yn wir, mae'n waradwydd i ddynoliaeth fod neb yn ymarferyd a'r fath ddicellion, hyd yn oed i ddinystrio eu gelynion . . .

(Foreign and Home News)

At the latest sessions in the town of Derby, two men were summoned before the court for selling Mr Paine's work *The Rights of Man*. The jury asked to read the book, and after studying it in detail, returned a verdict of Not guilty. A man in London (Mr Wood) was summoned before the court for printing Paine's Address to the Addressers — Lord Kenyon sent out the jurors twice to reconsider the case, and after a long wait on both occasions, they returned the verdict that the man was guilty of printing the book, but was not guilty of any offence. While some go free, many are being jailed for printing and selling the works of this man.

. . . It is said that the present war is costing this kingdom

£1,500 an hour . . . Behold the blessings of war!

. . . The parliament in Paris has declared Pitt an enemy of the human race.

. . . Marat a member of the Convention has been killed by Charlotte Corday . . . This Marat, it seems, was one of the leading Jacobins in Paris and possibly a man who wished well to his country.

. . . Now is the time for the allied armies to do their best to destroy France, because if the French can hold out for only a few months longer, they will possibly re-unite, and then it will be harder to conquer them than to stop the sun from rising . . . The letter from Pitt discovered in France has caused uncommon agitation in the Paris Convention; they say the government of England is behaving like a gang of criminals towards them, by sending in secret agents to turn France upside-down and to set the French to killing each other. If this story is true, it is a disgrace to humanity that anybody should resort to such vile trickery, even to destroy their enemies . . .

(21 August 1793. Extracts from the first news report to appear in the *Cylchgrawn Cymraeg* (*Welsh Journal*), edited by Morgan John Rhys, the first Welsh-language journal seriously to discuss political issues. *Cylchgrawn Cymraeg*, 3 Awst (August) 1793.)

D.4   All the thieves and whores of London are assembled about the fellow called Reeves and his fiddlers and faddlers in a mighty band, bawling and squawling like the Songs of Caterwauling, God-save-the-king, Church and King for ever! They press every one that passes by into this infernal service, crying to him — Blast your eyes! Cry Church and King! Church and King, damn your soul! I jabber'd Welsh, squeaked out Church SANS King in as broken a manner as I could and passed for a Dutchman.

(Iolo Morganwg on an encounter with the witch-hunting mobs of John Reeves, during the summer crisis of 1794, when *Habeas Corpus* was suspended and hundreds arrested, a crisis which reached its climax in Treason Trials in the autumn. [Dutchman = German.] National Library of Wales MS Iolo 837.)

D.5   My Lord Duke.

I am extremely sorry to acquaint your Grace with the following alarming Facts.

In pursuance of the Directions of the last Act of Parliament, for manning the Navy, my Brother Magistrates and I proceeded to carry it into Force, in the course of the last week, & issued our Orders to the several Parishes, thro' the County, accordingly.

The magistrates who reside in the neighbourhood of Denbigh, have, for some Time, held a regular monthly Meeting, upon the first Wednesday in the Month, being the Market Day, in that Town; in my way thither, this morning, some Friends met me, before I reached the Town, to apprize me that a very considerable Mob had assembled from the district, & adjoining my Parishes, to the amount of between 400, or 500 Persons, and are then in the Town, waiting for the Arrival of the Magistrates, two of the Gentlemen with whom I act being Clergymen it occurred to me, that they were, at the moment, attending, or doing Duty in their respective Churches; I therefore resolved to go on to Denbigh, to meet the Mob, & sent a Messenger to the eldest Mr Clough, to acquaint him with these circumstances, whenever he might arrive at Home, hoping that their assembling had been in consequence of their not being thoroughly acquainted with the Nature of the Act of Parliament, & that I could, by explaining it to them in their native Language, pacify them, & prevail upon them to disperse, but when I come to Denbigh, the Street was full of People to the amount I have stated, most of them armed with large Sticks, & Bludgeons, & upon my beginning to explain the Act to them, one John Jones of Aedryn, Farmer (who is supposed may be the Person whose name appears in the late Trials) told me, they did not want to have the Act explained to them, that Lord Camden had maintained in the House of Lords in the year 1775 or 1776 'that no Britton could be taxed without the Consent of the People'; the People became very unquiet, & used much seditious; & disagreeable Language, and I found too, that an Order had been issued, by the *Deputy Lieutenants* for holding a Meeting, on this Day, to ballot for men to serve in the Militia, in the Room of those who had died since the last Meetings, and that the High Constables had, ignorantly, issued their Precepts to the several Parishes (not having regard to those Parishes only, in which the vacancies had fallen out) and that this Proceeding had excited the present Alarm amongst the People: but I have my Suspicions that these Lists were the Fabrication of some seditious men, who took this Mode of stirring up Discontent amongst the Ignorant stating to them, that a new, & general Ballot was intended; it was in vain to expostulate with them, they were determined to resist the raising of any more men for the Militia, or the Mareens as they stiled them, meaning, no Doubt, the late Act for manning the Navy. Some of the Ringleaders of the Mob threatened me bodily Hurt, & that they would pull down my Houses, stone by stone, as well as those of my Colleagues if we attempted to carry either of the lists into Execution, seven or 8 of them laid hold of My Horse's Head, Stirrups, etc.etc.and John Jones pretended to wish me well, & advised me to comply with the Requests made by the Mob, or he did not know the Consequences of a Refusal; after about an Hour spent in this manner, the Revd Mr Thos. Clough came up the Town, & met me, when the Mob surrounded him, and laid hold of his Horse in like Manner, & conducted him, & me up to the Crown Inn. Mr Clough alighted from his Horse, & went up into one of the Rooms above Stairs, accompanied by a great Number of the Mob, & I continued on Horseback at the Door, and before the Window of the Room in which Mr Clough was, & upon the Mob requiring a Paper, under our Hands, that we would not proceed to enforce either the Militia or *Navy Act*, we complied with the Proposal, seeing it was in Vain to avoid it, when a Stamped Piece of Paper was brought to me, & I wrote that Mr Clough & I undertook, and promised, that we would use our endeavours to prevent any more Men being ballotted for, etc. etc., the Paper was read to them, translated into Welsh and John Jones was called upon to peruse it, he seeming all the Time to be the Person the Mob looked up to, and he suggested an Amendment including the late *Navy Act*, which I at his Request, & Diction, interlined; the Paper was then sent upstairs for Mr Clough's Signature, and some other Amendment was suggested by John Jones, which he was dictating, & Mr Clough writing, when I went into the Room, by the direction of the Mob. In a short time Mr Roger Butler Clough arrived at the House, & the Mob then insisted upon his signing the Paper which he did after much Debate amongst the Leaders it was resolved that one Paper was sufficient, some of them having proposed that a Paper should be given to each Parish, which Point was at length given up, & John Jones was fixed upon to keep the Paper; this having been complied with, some of the Mob demanded Money, as Payment for their Loss of Time, & to procure Meat & Drink, one proposing that we should give them 5*s.* a Parish, which was accordingly done . . .

(1 April 1795. A magistrate's account of the crowd's seizure of the town of Denbigh during the widespread riots, crowd actions and rebellions which convulsed much of western Wales in the crisis of that year and the next over food shortages, conscription and the war. J. Lloyd, Wigfair — Home and War Offices, HO 42/34/191.)

D.6   O FRANCE: although I do not justify thy excesses, I venerate thy magnanimity . . . INVINCIBLE FRENCHMEN! go on! . . . The Popish beast has numbered his days! . . . Infatuated Britons! I feel for your insanity, although four thousand miles from your coast . . . ANCIENT BRITONS! awake out of sleep! Open your eyes! Why are your tyrants great? Because you kneel down and cringe to them. Rise up. You are their equals! If you cannot rise, creep to the ocean and the friendly waves will waft you over the Atlantic to the hospitable shores of America . . . Quit the little despotic island which gave you birth and leave the tyrants and the slaves of your country to live and die together . . .

(1795, 4 July Oration by Morgan John Rhys at Greenville (later Ohio), site of Indian Peace talks, published by the St David's Society of Philadelphia in 1798 and dispatched in bulk to Wales. Historical Society of Pennsylvania, Philadelphia, USA.)

D.7   The only news that this country affords is that a vessel sails from Carnarvon to America this month with about 300 Emigrants all Inhabitants of Carnarvonshire, Anglesey or Denbighshire.

(Robert Williams, Llandudno, to William Owen, 21 January 1796. National Library of Wales MS 13224, fo.161–2.)

D.8 Where is this new country which you are going to secure to the Welsh and how are the poor moneyless emigrants to get thither? . . . I recommend the bearer of this, Theophilus Rees, a man with a competent share of property but with the disadvantage of knowing but little English. He and his family of eleven are leaving with many *Baptists* . . . together with a number of *Presbyterians* and other serious people to the number of six or seven score . . . would that I could join them in your happy country, but I am forced to return to hateful England . . .

(William Richards (Lynn), St Clears, to Dr Samuel Jones, Philadelphia, 22 March 1796. Pennepek papers, USA [Presbyterian = Unitarian].)

D.9 Court of Great Sessions, Montgomeryshire. The jurors present. That John Ellis, late of the parish of Llanbrynmair in the county of Montgomeryshire, yeoman, being a pernicious and seditious man and contriving and intending the liege Subjects of our said Lord the King to incite and move to hatred and dislike of the Person of our said Lord the King and the Government established within this Realm on the Seventeenth Day of December in the 37th Year of the Reign of our Sovereign Lord, King George III [1796] . . . the said John Ellis then and there was talking of and concerning the Government of our said Lord the King unlawfully, maliciously and wickedly did publish, utter and declare with a Loud Voice these Welsh words following, to wit . . . I mae yr Tylawd yn cail eu gwascu gan y Cywaithog ag i mae ne wedi resolvio y gael rheiolaeth arall ag ny dydiw ddim yn power Gwirboneddigion y wlad ei rhwystro ne ag ys gwna nhw fe geiff fod yn waed am waed . . . which Welsh words bear the same meaning as the following English words . . . The Poor are oppressed by the Rich and we are determined to have another Government and it is not in the power of the Gentlemen of the Country to prevent it, if they do, it shall be blood for blood . . .

[17 December 1796. An incident during the sustained disturbances thoughout Merioneth and Montgomeryshire over the winter of 1796–7, which were triggered by the new Militia Act of November 1796, but which broadened in scope and became 'subversive'. For three months, the region around Llanbrynmair in particular witnessed many outrages and mass meetings hostile to the government; a number of small farmers of the parish were indicted for 'raising insurrection'.]

(National Library of Wales MS Great Sessions, Montgomeryshire 1797, Gaol Files 4/196/1.)

D.10 Breeches, petticoats, shirts, blankets, sheets (for some received the news in bed) have been most woefully defiled in South Wales lately on hearing that a thimblefull of Frenchmen landed on our coast . . . Our Dragooners sent us some companies of Dragoons after the old women of Pembrokeshire had secured the damned Republicans as it seems we are requested to call them. Are there no lamp-irons in Downing Street? I fear that the hemp crop of the last season failed. We must allow that the French are beforehand with us in the most useful arts and sciences, witness their invention and use of the guillotine . . .

(7 March 1797. Iolo Morganwg's comment on the French landing at Fishguard. Lamp-irons (street lamp standards) were what the Parisian populace favoured for the lynching of bishops and other undesirables; hemp provided the English gallows-rope. Iolo Morganwg to William Owen Pughe, National Library of Wales MS 13222, fo.131–4.)

D.11 I am a Jacobin and a Republican and know a Republican Government would be a much better one than the present and I'll lay a wager that there will not be a Crowned Head in Europe in three years' time and that there will soon be a change in our Government.

(23 June 1800. Great Sessions, Anglesey. John Phillips, small farmer of Llangefni, quoted as making a public declaration at Llannerch-y-medd. 'Seditious' pamphlets had been circulated in Llannerch-y-medd during the crisis of 1796. During the even more serious crisis of 1800–1, which forced the Peace of

Amiens, 'Republican principles' had been widely disseminated through north-west Wales, directed at small farmers reacting against the Militia Act and the grain crisis. University College of North Wales, Porth yr Aur, Add. MS 2060 and Plas Newydd correspondence, II, 3551–4.)

D.12 The bearer of this, Daniel Davis, is about to emigrate to your country with his wife and seven children. He is by trade a mason and understands the farming business pretty well . . . his wife has had some education and has sometimes kept school . . . Two of her brothers are in the ministry in England among the *Presbyterians* . . . I am ashamed to trouble you and Dr Rogers so often with the concerns of these poor Emigrants, but what in God's name can I do? . . . I cannot describe to you the condition of our poor country, thousands of the poor move about the country begging bread . . . Myriads would emigrate if they had money . . .

(William Richards (Lynn), Newcastle Emlyn, to Dr Samuel Jones, Philadelphia, April 1801. Pennepek Papers, USA.)

D.13 An Address to the Workmen of Merthyr Tydvil
The present high price of the necessaries of Life is gone to such enormous rate that we the workmen of the Ironworks on the Hills have come to the following resolutions, that they are determined to assemble on a certain day, to consider of the most effectual method to be adopted in extricating ourselves and the rising Generation from the Tyranny and Oppression of the times for it is evident to the shallowest understanding that it is sure to go worse and worse for every new Tax that is laid on us, is sure to raise the Price of the articles that are taxt, which we makes no doubt but what you will freely admit. So we hopes that you will join us in the above desirable undertaking, so necessary to the happiness and preservation of the human race and rescue ourselves and the succeeding Generation from the most daring, insulting and atrocious Tyranny, so dont lose no time in concerting measures to collect yourselves together in a mass and be all of one mind as one man, and there will be no doubt of our success for the Tyrants will not be able to face us,

for their guilty consciences will make them tremble with fear, altho they puts such trust in the military force of those kingdoms but it can never be supposed that an army of natives will fight to keep their Fathers and Mothers, Sisters and Brothers and all their relations in a state of Slavery and Misery and it will fall to their own Lot as soon as they are discharged from the Service, we was all in hopes that you would a come over that way when you rose lately and if you had we should a Completed that great work of reformation before this time and should be a people at once free and happy, we have concluded that M-a-y- D-a-y [*sic*] shall be the time for the Farmers will have all their Corn in the Ground and there will be no fear of famine if the Almighty will be pleased to send us a good harvest — Next Sunday or the following one is the time. There is a great many men that believes that the King has no power, but what is given him by parliament, it tis true, that it twas intended that it should be so in the beginning, but the Case is alterd very much for he and his Ministry has got all the power, and both houses of parliament are no more than a shadow or an image for he has got such means to bribe and corrupt them, so that the major part of them will give their Votes with him, Let him propose what he will, So when he sends a Bill towards raising supplies for the Current Year he is sure to find a Majority for they are sure to find there is a part of it to themselves and it is not unreasonable to suppose when a prince has got Thirty Seven or Thirty Eight millions a year of revenues from his subjects that it is his interest to bribe a few in order that he might be enabled to fleece the rest for his Ministers and Privy Counsellors and a great part of both Houses of parliament are in places of profits and emolument, so that and the rest live in hopes of arriving at preferments themselves, so that they dont care how they the rest of their fellow Creatures does so they do gain their point, but it tis quite against the true intent and meaning of the people that they represent for the representatives of the people ought to be a set of men wholly impartial, both to King and People and not take Bribes for their Votes, Nor to complain of the grievances if there did none exist, but they are become unlawful assembly, and ought to be deposed as well as him that has corrupted them, and a new form of government Established upon *Whig*

Principles or any other that may be adopted after the sense of the
Nation is taken on the subject . . .

(Quoted in David J.V. Jones, *Before Rebecca: Popular Protests in
Wales 1793–1835*, London, 1973, pp.213–5.)

Debating the Evidence

Gwyn A. Williams writes an eloquent essay on the beginnings of Welsh
Radicalism, a subject which he has done so much to illuminate,
especially in its transatlantic dimension. He has restored the *Madoc*
legend to its proper place in Welsh history (*Madoc: the Making of a Myth*,
London, 1979) and he has uncovered the close connections which
existed between radical *Dissenters* in Wales and their counterparts in the
newly independent United States of America (*The Search for Beulah Land*,
London, 1980). It is fascinating, indeed heady, stuff and its importance
as the origin of a major tradition in modern Welsh politics is immense.

Source D.1
William Jones's message to his fellow countrymen is not made explicit in
this extract — but it is surely clear enough. What are the implications of
what he says?

Source D.2
What were to be the main characteristics of the colony which *Iolo
Morganwg* proposed should be established near the Mississippi? Can it be
a coincidence that it was in this general area that the 'Welsh Indians'
were then thought to live?

Source D.3
It is relevant to ask if this is a primary source for the events reported.
Perhaps more important is the fact that this is the first example of radical
political journalism in the Welsh language. For the first time monoglot
Welshmen could read of such matters in their own language.

Source D.4
What is the historical value of a passage such as this? (One need not
assume that every detail is literally true. See Source D.10 for another of
Iolo Morganwg's colourfully phrased letters).

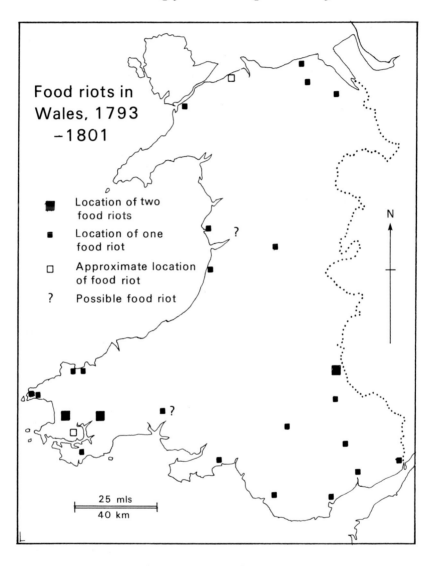

Food riots in
Wales, 1793
–1801

■ Location of two
food riots

■ Location of one
food riot

□ Approximate location
of food riot

? Possible food riot

N

25 mls
40 km

Source D.5

Are there any reasons for thinking that the squire and magistrate, John Lloyd, sent a reasonably accurate account of these proceedings at Denbigh to the Home Secretary? What queries should one have in mind when handling evidence of this kind? Consider carefully the role of John Jones of Aeddryn in the Denbigh riot.

Source D.6

Perhaps Fourth of July speeches always tend to the rhetorical. Morgan John Rhys's view of the state of things in Wales may be justifiable, but what is one to make of 'the friendly waves will waft you over the Atlantic'? Note Professor Williams's comment about 'hideous crossings which cost half the lives on board'. Is such a speech likely to have had much influence in encouraging emigration from Wales to the United States?

Sources D.6, D.7 and D.8

These extracts illustrate the exodus of Welsh people to America following the crisis of 1795. They also underline Professor Williams's point about the close contacts which already existed between the *Dissenters* on either side of the Atlantic. (Also compare Source D.12, dated 1801.)

Source D.9

This is a presentment of the Grand Jury of Montgomeryshire, at that time an essential preliminary to a criminal trial. In archaic and highly charged language the Grand Jury states that there is a case to be answered, and the trial of John Ellis would follow. This is not therefore a statement of facts proved in court, much less a verdict. Nevertheless, it seems likely enough that John Ellis did utter the stirring Welsh words alleged.

Source D.10

Iolo Morganwg is both indecent and seditious in this private letter to his friend William Owen Pughe; he would have been in serious trouble had the authorities intercepted it. Written about a fortnight after the farcical episode of the landing of the French near Fishguard and their defeat by the 'old women of Pembrokeshire', the letter exhibits the exaggerated response of an out-and-out radical. Can one believe that he really

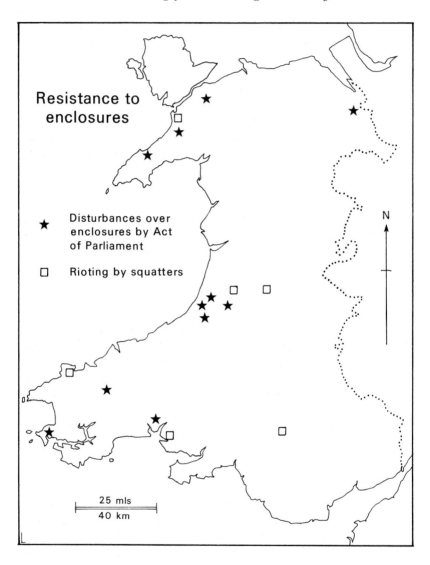

Resistance to enclosures

★   Disturbances over enclosures by Act of Parliament

☐   Rioting by squatters

25 mls
40 km

advocated executions on lamp posts and the guillotine? What was the reaction of the majority of Welsh people to the French invasion?

Source D.11

Sources D.5, D.9 and D.11 illustrate the radical views of people in widely separated parts of rural, Welsh-speaking Wales in the 1790s. Compare also the views of *William Jones* of Llangadfan given in Source D.1 and in Source B.21 in the chapter on 'New Enthusiasts'. Comment on the penetration of radical ideas into the remotest areas of the country following the American and French revolutions.

Source D.12

This letter of 1801 re-emphasizes the point to be gleaned from Sources D.6, D.7 and D.8 about the transatlantic dimension of Welsh *Dissent*; this connection facilitated emigration to the United States. Note in particular the *Presbyterian* connection in the light of what Professor Williams says about the radicalism of that denomination.

Source D.13

What strikes you about the style of this cry of the workmen of Merthyr? The American and French revolutions and the writings of Tom Paine provided the ideology, the misery of food shortage and soaring prices in 1800–1 provided the seed-bed. The radicalism of rural Wales in the 1790s was short-lived (it did not revive until the middle of the nineteenth century), but this document from the heart of industrial Wales is truly the start of a political tradition which is dominant even now.

Discussion

The thirteen sources which have been selected mostly date from the 1790s — the decade which Gwyn A. Williams elsewhere describes as 'an intellectual cauldron of competing ideologies in Wales' (*When was Wales?*, Penguin edition, Harmondsworth, 1985, p.152). The documents have been chosen to illustrate the ferment among certain sections of the Welsh population and of the London Welsh in the wake of the American and French revolutions; they also show the unrest which existed in most parts of Wales in consequence of the social and economic dislocations of the period of the French wars (1793–1815).

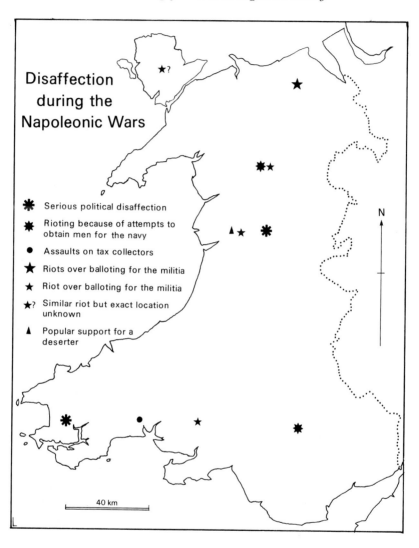

Disaffection during the Napoleonic Wars

* Serious political disaffection
* Rioting because of attempts to obtain men for the navy
● Assaults on tax collectors
★ Riots over balloting for the militia
★ Riot over balloting for the militia
★? Similar riot but exact location unknown
▲ Popular support for a deserter

40 km

Riots were endemic in the 1790s, and especially so in the critical years 1795–6 and 1800–1; they occurred in market towns, in industrial districts and in the countryside. Their causes were oppression, misery and hunger, and their spokesmen were beginning to voice a radical ideology. Political ideas of the American and French revolutionaries (prominent among the philosophers of these revolutions were the Welshmen *Richard Price* and *David Williams*), and the writings of Tom Paine (*The Rights of Man*, 1790–2, mediated through the Welsh language by *Jac Glan-y-gors*), had penetrated to the remotest parts of the north and west.

But one should be careful to place this evidence in a broad context. The radicals were few in number in the 1790s and they mostly belonged to the 'left wing' of *Dissent* (Nonconformity) — people such as *Iolo Morganwg*, William Richards of Lynn and Morgan John Rhys. They were men who were moving towards *Unitarianism* and rationalism in theology. They formed what Professor Williams (following the Italian Antonio Gramsci) calls an 'organic intelligentsia'. The majority of *Dissenters* in Wales — together with the *Methodists*, by whom they were greatly influenced — were of a quite different cast: evangelical, *Calvinist*, absorbed in religious and spiritual concerns, quietist if not *Tory* in politics.

The formal political structure too was only slightly affected by the radical movement of the late eighteenth century. The old-style, gentry-dominated parliamentary politics dating from the Acts of Union in the sixteenth century was still in place. (See Philip Jenkins's analysis of this in his chapter 'Political Quiescence and Political Ferment'.) *Dissent*, Radicalism, industrialization and the rise of a wealthy new class of capitalists and professional men, all these things were pressing against the bastions of the traditional political families in the 1790s, but it was several decades before there was any major yielding of power. The election of Benjamin Hall, son-in-law of the Cyfarthfa ironmaster Richard Crawshay, as member for Glamorgan in 1814 was the first outward sign of change.

Portrait of Lady Llanover (1802–96) painted by Mornewicke in 1862. (*Source: National Museum of Wales.*)

Mythology and Tradition

R. PAUL EVANS

The eighteenth century was characterized in Wales by a series of changes which transformed the whole fabric of traditional Welsh life and society. The quickening pace of change which resulted from the agricultural and industrial revolutions, and from the religious and educational revivals of the period, encouraged a cultural awakening or renaissance. The gradual decay throughout the century of an ancient and customary way of life stimulated Welsh scholars to make a last desperate bid to recover and revive as much as possible of their ancient history, language, literature and culture before it disappeared for ever. This sense of urgency to obtain a permanent record of a vanishing culture is seen in Dr William Owen Pughe's editorial preface to the first volume of *The Cambrian Register* of 1796 (E.1). Pughe exclaimed that, although Wales possessed a vast treasure of literary and oral tradition, scarcely a morsel had been recorded for posterity, and this recovery of ancient lore was now the most urgent and pressing task facing Welsh scholars.

E.1

In his analysis of this cultural renaissance, historian Prys Morgan has shown that what began in the middle decades of the century as a scholarly and methodical attempt to recover past tradition, increasingly became tinged with an element of fantasy and, in some instances, even forgery, and culminated in the late eighteenth and early nineteenth centuries in the deliberate invention of tradition. This trend towards the imaginative and creative is well illustrated in the field of Welsh literature, particularly in a comparison of the printed works of the Reverend *Evan Evans*, 'Ieuan Fardd', and *Edward Williams*, 'Iolo Morganwg'. In 1758 *Lewis Morris*, the eldest of the three Morris brothers of Anglesey, wrote with great excitement to his friend Edward Richard of Ystrad Meurig to inform him that his protégé, *Evan Evans*, had just rediscovered, in some old manuscripts, the sixth-century poetry of *Aneirin* (E.2). To *Lewis Morris* this was as great a discovery for Welsh literature as was the discovery of America by Columbus, for it proved beyond any doubt that Wales had its own distinct historical tradition which could be traced back through generations. In 1764 Evans published the fruits of his research in *Some Specimens of the Poetry of the Antient Welsh Bards*, which was a scholarly survey of Welsh poetry from the sixth to the sixteenth century. In 1773 the literary squire of Blaenau, Rice Jones, continued this process of recovery by publishing his *Gorchestion Beirdd Cymru* (*Exploits of the Welsh Bards*), which comprised a selection of the poetic works of *Aneirin*, *Taliesin* and *Llywarch Hen*.

E.2

Such scholarly works were the result of many years of painstaking research, but to some Welsh patriots, and especially to *Iolo Morganwg*, this slow, methodical and rather piecemeal recovery of material was far too limited, and in Iolo's opinion did little to excite the curiosity of the populace at large. What was needed, Iolo believed, was a more dramatic and lively picture of the past and so he deliberately and self-consciously set about trying to create such an image. The son of a stonemason from Flemingston in the Vale of Glamorgan, Iolo possessed a quite extraordinary passion for Welsh history and literature. A lifelong addict to the drug *laudanum*, he has been described by Prys Morgan as 'the rogue elephant' of the literary tradition, whose forgeries present a perfect example of how the process of cultural recovery ran out of control.

When, in 1789, William Owen Pughe edited *Barddoniaeth Dafydd ab Gwilym*, a collection of poems by the fourteenth-century poet *Dafydd ap Gwilym*, the work contained an appendix of some twenty hitherto unknown poems by Dafydd which had been forwarded to Pughe by Iolo, who claimed he had transcribed them from some obscure Glamorgan manuscripts. In fact the poems were Iolo's own forgeries, but of such a convincing standard that it was not until the middle decades of this century that Welsh academics were finally able to distinguish them from the original. In the late 1790s Iolo was

appointed as one of the editors of the *Myvyrian Archaiology of
Wales*, a work intended to be a repository of medieval Welsh
literature collected from a variety of old manuscripts (E.3).
Three volumes were published between 1801 and 1807, the
second and third volumes of which contained a considerable
proportion of bogus material invented by Iolo. Indeed the third
volume, which was by far the most popular with the public in
the nineteenth century, was entirely of Iolo's own concoction,
although this was not suspected until long afterwards. But this
deliberate invention of tradition was not peculiar to Wales
alone, and should be viewed as part of a more general romantic
revival which encompassed the whole of western Europe. In
Scotland, for instance, James Macpherson published trans-
lations of Gaelic poems in 1762–3 which he alleged had been
originally composed in the third century by a Celtic poet named
Ossian, but which in reality were Macpherson's own bogus
compositions.

A similar picture of romantic mythologizing can be seen in
the revival of the *eisteddfod* in the late eighteenth century.
Although this institution had a long history which could be
traced back to a meeting of professional bards at Cardigan
Castle in 1176, by the end of the sixteenth century the *eisteddfod*
was in a state of serious decline. In 1694 the last of the
professional household bards died, and the small parochial
eisteddfodau which emerged after this date were little more than
the gatherings of a handful of amateur poets who met to recite
their compositions over a pint of ale at the local tavern, and
hence they became known as '*eisteddfod* y dafarn'. Notifications
of meetings were sometimes printed in Welsh almanacs as were
some of the winning compositions. When, in 1734, the aged
poet and publisher Siôn Rhydderch attended an *eisteddfod* at
Dolgellau he was bitterly disappointed at the extremely poor
attendance (E.4), which he blamed on the lack of gentry
patronage and on the decline of the Welsh language. To
Rhydderch there seemed little hope of any revival unless the
then current trend of decline and apathy could be reversed, and
some form of patronage and encouragement found.

In the event it is not until 1789 that it is possible to detect any
large-scale revival, when in that year three important *eisteddfodau*

were held in north-east Wales. The initiative was taken by two local patriots, the poet Jonathan Hughes of Llangollen and the exciseman Thomas Jones of Corwen, but the overall success of the venture was due to the encouragement and financial assistance received from the London-based *Gwyneddigion* Society, which was a kind of cultural and convivial club for north Walians residing in the capital. In January 1789 Hughes organized an *eisteddfod* at Llangollen but because of the winter weather few poets attended, and in the following month he wrote to the *Gwyneddigion* Society appealing for their support to help organize a further meeting later in the year (E.5). The *Gwyneddigion* responded to the challenge and the *eisteddfodau* held at Corwen in May and at Bala in September were a great success, and ushered in a newly prosperous era for the institution (E.6). To attract a wider audience new methods were adopted and competitions for singers and instrumentalists, events which had not been staged since Tudor times, were added to the traditional poetic contests. At the St Asaph *Eisteddfod* for 1791 a *penillion*-singing contest lasted some thirteen hours, much to the amusement of the audience. Medals, which were specially designed by the renowned French sculptor Dupré, were provided by the *Gwyneddigion*. Thus what was 'rediscovered' in 1789 was a judicious blend of the old and the new, of ancient tradition and ceremonial combining with myth and innovation in an attempt to revitalize the institution and provide it with a more popular following.

The success of the revived *eisteddfod* in north-east Wales aroused the jealousy of *Iolo Morganwg* who, in a deliberate attempt to prove that his native region of south Wales could lay claim to similar ancient ceremonial, invented the now familiar 'Order of the Bards of the Island of Great Britain'. He claimed that this '*Gorsedd*', or guild of bards, was part of an ancient druidic ritual which had survived only in the remote hills of Glamorgan and that he and Edward Evan of Aberdare were the last of the druidic bards, hence the necessity of making public this ceremony. He held his first public gathering on Primrose Hill in London on 21 June 1792, and saw to it that accounts of the meeting were published in leading newspapers and journals (E.7). Iolo claimed that this ceremony could be traced back virtually unchanged for some two thousand years, and although the whole affair captured the fertile imagination of members of the *Gwyneddigion*, not all scholars were entirely convinced. One such sceptic was John Walters of Llandough who wrote to E.8   Edward Davies in 1792 (E.8) expressing his belief that Iolo's ideas on bardism were a 'made dish' composed of nothing but 'wild invention'. Nevertheless, in 1819, Iolo was successful in having the ceremony of the *Gorsedd* incorporated into the *eisteddfod* proceedings at Carmarthen, for which he invented an array of robes, ritual and regalia, although the present *Gorsedd* regalia dates from the late nineteenth century. It is somewhat ironic that what today is regarded by millions as the most traditional and ancient of ceremonies in the National *Eisteddfod*, is in essence pure fantasy, the result of one man's extraordinary desire to create an appealing and coherent image of the past.

The eighteenth century witnessed a revival of interest in ancient bardic and druidic lore, and this helped to create an atmosphere in which Iolo's *Gorsedd* appeared quite plausible and acceptable. Following the accession of the Tudors in 1485 Wales lost its own distinct historical tradition, which was absorbed instead into British dynastic history. It was not until 1707 that the philologist *Edward Lhuyd* provided the Welsh with a new and quite independent vision of their past when he proved that the Welsh language was related to Cornish, Breton, Irish and Gaelic, and that they could all be traced back to a common ancestor which he termed 'Celtic'. The ideas put forward by Lhuyd and by the Breton abbot, Paul-Yves Pezron, acted as a catalyst in stimulating interest in Celtic tradition, particularly into the activities of the Druids, the Celtic religious priests. The contribution of Lhuyd and Pezron was recognized E.9   by the Reverend Henry Rowlands of Llanidan (E.9), who has been dubbed 'the Welsh *Stukeley*' for his pioneering work in rehabilitating the image of the druidic order. In 1723 Rowlands published his *Mona Antiqua Restaurata*, in which he attempted to show that Anglesey had been the heartland of the druidic order E.10   (E.10). He based his assumptions upon crude place name derivations such as Tre'r Dryw, which he dubiously translated as 'the Town of the Druids', and upon the archaeological remains of *megalithic* stone monuments which he believed to be

An Arch Druid in His Judicial Habit, a coloured aquatint from S.R. Meyrick and C.H. Smith, *The Costume of the Original Inhabitants of the British Islands, 1815. (Source: BBC Hulton Picture Library.)*

the remnants of druidic altars and temples. He did much to popularize the image of the ancient druidic priest, and his work helped usher in a period of 'druidomania' in the late eighteenth century.

Tourists, clearly inspired by the ideas of Rowlands, scoured the Isle of Anglesey in search of druidic remains (E.11, E.12), while several were accompanied by artists who were commissioned to paint scenes of the ruined altars and temples. Antiquarians and historians such as Richard Colt Hoare and Richard Fenton delighted in images of the ancient druids, and were enthusiastic excavators of burial mounds and tombs. In his *Historical Tour through Pembrokeshire* (1811), Fenton makes frequent reference to druidic remains, as for instance in his description of the village of Drewson (E.13), which he claimed was corrupted from 'Druidstown' and which had once possessed a *Gorsedd* stone circle. Edward Davies, nicknamed 'Celtic Davies', published his *Celtic Researches* in 1804 and *The Mythology and Rites of the British Druids* in 1809, in which he put forward fanciful ideas on druidic lore, and yet at the same time doubted the authenticity of Iolo's *Gorsedd* of the Bards.

Another aspect of this revival of interest in past tradition was the emergence in the late eighteenth century of a number of national folk heroes, some based upon sound historical fact, others upon pure fantasy. In the 1770s the scholars *Evan Evans* and *Thomas Pennant* portrayed Owain Glyndŵr for the first time as a great Welsh national hero, not as the half-mad traitor and rebel to the English crown of previous depiction. By the end of the century English tourists were referring to the Dee Valley as 'Glendower Country', and his portrait was celebrated on the billboards of inns and hotels in the area. The English poet *Thomas Gray* made famous, in one of the most celebrated poems of the eighteenth century, the story of the Welsh bard who, in order to escape the massacre of his colleagues ordered by *Edward I* shortly after 1282, flung himself from the top of a great precipice into the River Conwy (E.14). Although purely imaginary, *Gray*'s 'Bard' became a popular figure in the 1770s and 1780s, particularly among English tourists who flocked to the hills above Conwy to view the spot where the supposed incident had taken place (E.15). It was also the theme for several

E.11
E.12

E.13

E.14

E.15

famous paintings by *Paul Sandby*, *Philippe de Loutherbourg* and *Thomas Jones* of Pencerrig. In a blatant attempt to encourage English tourists to visit north Wales, one enterprising hotel-owner from Beddgelert invented the legend in the 1780s that the village had obtained its name from the grave of Gelert, a greyhound which had been mistakenly killed by its master, Prince *Llywelyn the Great*. By the time Michael Faraday toured Wales in 1819 he could record in his journal that the story of E.16 Gelert was familiar to everyone (E.16), and in 1811 it was made the subject of a famous poem by William Spencer. Today it is a story well known to all Welsh schoolchildren, and is a good example of how easily wild invention became mistaken for actual tradition.

The most remarkable of all these mythical creations was the story of *Madoc* ap Owain Gwynedd, a twelfth-century prince who, it was claimed, had discovered America in 1170 some three hundred years before Columbus. The myth had first made its appearance during the Tudor period, but received a second and more formidable revival in the 1790s when '*Madoc* fever' hit the London Welsh. In 1791 reports were received of the discovery on the banks of the Missouri of a group of Indians called 'Mandans' or 'Padoucas', who were said to be the direct descendants of *Madoc* and who still spoke Welsh. David Samwell, the Welsh surgeon and prominent member of the *Gwyneddigion* Society, who had accompanied Captain Cook on his circumnavigation of the globe, was entirely convinced by E.17 the story, as indeed were many London Welshmen (E.17). The *Gwyneddigion*, spurred on by *Iolo Morganwg* who had forged documents to help corroborate the claim, agreed to finance an expedition to search out the Mandan Indians, which was to be led by the young John Evans of Waunfawr near Caernarfon E.18 (E.18). After a long and dangerous trek Evans reached the Mandan Indians in 1786 only to discover that they were not Welsh-speaking. Nevertheless, the story of *Madoc* became a powerful legend, and when, in 1858, Thomas Stephens of Merthyr Tydfil produced an award-winning essay on *Madoc* at the Llangollen *Eisteddfod*, he was not awarded a prize because his essay proved that *Madoc* could not have discovered America.

Associated with this movement to provide the Welsh with a

sense of identity and nationality was the emergence of a vast array of signs, symbols and regalia. Mention has already been made of the association of *cromlechs* and *megaliths* with druidic altars, and in 1751, when *Lewis Morris* designed a banner for the newly created Cymmrodorion Society of London Welshmen, he chose, as the two supporting figures to the coat of arms and symbols, the Ancient Druid and St David. The druid appeared on the title pages of many books on Wales, while *Iolo Morganwg* did much to cultivate the myth of the bardic circle or *Gorsedd*. The harp, the leek and the wild mountain goat also emerged as representative symbols of Welsh tradition, as did the three ostrich plumes of the Prince of Wales. In the early nineteenth century the red dragon became a popular symbol, while in the 1830s Augusta Waddington, Lady Llanover, created what is now considered to be the traditional national costume of Wales, consisting of a large red cloak and a tall black hat. The cultivation of this wealth of insignia served to embody a strong cultural and nationalistic awareness of past tradition.

The English tourists, who visited Wales in ever-increasing numbers from about 1770 onwards, also helped to create a new image of Wales as a land of picturesque beauty, romantic charm and quaintness. The Reverend William Gilpin, who toured the south in 1770 and the north in 1773, delighted in the picturesque

E.19   scenes which confronted him upon his travels (E.19), while landscape painters began to portray the mountainous regions of Wales as areas of great natural beauty. The native-born artist Richard Wilson made famous through his oil paintings such scenes as 'Llyn Peris and Dolbadarn Castle', 'Snowdon from Llyn Nantlle', and 'Llyn-y-Cae under Cader Idris'. So well known did Wilson's landscapes become shortly after his death in 1782, that travellers came to refer to Llyn-y-Cau as 'Wilson's Pool'. Together, both travel writer and painter created a new image of Wales as a land of great historical interest and natural beauty, a tradition which has remained to the present day, but which is a far cry indeed from the very harsh and often abusive criticisms recorded by the few English travellers who had

E.20   visited Wales earlier in that century (E.20).

Thus the movement towards the recovery and revival of past tradition should be seen as part of an attempt to provide the

The druidic priest as portrayed by the Revd Henry Rowlands in his *Mona Antiqua Restaurata*, 1723.

Welsh with a sense of identity and nationality. Where that recovery of actual tradition proved to be inadequate or unappealing, then Welsh patriots were not averse to enlivening the story by adding an element of fantasy or invention. In essence, it was the adaptation of myth and tradition to suit a changing society which was involved in a desperate bid to uncover its roots.

Sources

E.1   Since the revival of learning in Europe, most nations have been emulous of bringing forward their respective stores of ancient memorials, in order to enrich the common stock; but a vast treasure is contained in the Welsh language, in manuscripts, and the oral traditions of the people, of which barely a notice has hitherto been given to the world.

To investigate this hidden repository, and to bring to light whatever may be deemed most rare and valuable, is the primary object of the following work.

(William Owen Pughe's editorial preface to the first volume of *The Cambrian Register*, 1796.)

E.2   Who do you think I have at my elbow, as happy as ever Alexander thought himself after a conquest? No less a man than Ieuan Fardd [*Evan Evans*], who hath discovered some old MSS lately that no body of this age or the last ever as much as dreamed of. And this discovery is to him and me as great as that of America by Columbus. We have found an epic Poem in the British [Welsh] called Gododin, equal at least to the *Iliad*, *Aeneid* or *Paradise Lost*. Tudfwlch and Marchlew are heroes fiercer than Achilles and Satan.

(Hugh Owen (ed.), *Additional Letters of the Morrises of Anglesey, 1735–1786*, London, 1947, I, p.349.)

E.3   The existence of very ancient Welsh Manuscripts, in prose and verse, has been announced considerably more than two centuries ago: many respectable English writers have expressed a degree of surprise, and even regret, that these valuable remains of antiquity have never been consigned to the press; and so long have their expectations been disappointed, that hints, and even assertions, have of late been thrown out, that we have none, or none that are authentic; we will however advise such as entertain this opinion to suspend their judgment until the completion of this publication.

(Iolo's introductory essay to the first volume of *The Myvyrian Archaiology of Wales*, London, 1801.)

E.4   I travelled over eighty miles from the furthest part of South Wales, in high hopes of meeting most of the poets of Wales who had some talent in Verse. But not half a dozen came in all, or at least it did not appear more. Be that as it may, as I saw there only signs of apathy, faint-heartedness and cowardice. And because of lack of help and aspersions to the art, I fear that some failing, or rather, as it were her decline from the language and art of our grandfathers, the noblemen of which were formerly very helpful to the matter, as it plainly appears by the number of them who were in the great *eisteddfod* at Caerwys [1567], and many other *eisteddfodau*. For my part, I shall not bother my head any more about such a thing . . . .

(Siôn Rhydderch's [John Roderick] introduction to his *Almanac* for 1735.)

E.5   The old customs are now held in low regard, because they are so uncommon. However, the crowd which came together were well pleased with the clumsy poesy that was there, so much that they ordained another *eisteddfod* at Corwen in Merioneth to be on May 12th next, expecting more bards to come there, and many promise to come there, but what stops many is poverty. Many are held back by worldliness, others by faintheartedness, for there is neither profit nor advantage from such a custom, so everyone is very slack and dragging their feet, and slow to build or to beautify or to extend the bounds of the Welsh language, and now we, the few natives here, greet you and believe that there is in you some remains of the spirit of Fraternity. We would beg for your patronage if you would be pleased to give us some small present, out of goodwill to those who are trying to crawl after their Mother tongue . . . Perhaps we may bit by bit come to walk — for children are enticed to walk by a few toys.

(Translation of a letter sent by Jonathan Hughes of Llangollen to the Gwyneddigion Society of London on 25th February 1789. Quoted by G.J. Williams in 'Llythyrau ynglyn ag eisteddfodau'r Gwyneddigion', *Llen Cymru*, I, 1950, p.29.)

E.6   [The meeting at Corwen] . . . gave a zest to the encouragement of native talent, and another [meeting] was immediately advertised to be held, by the Society [*Gwyneddigion*], at Bala, on the 29th and 30th September following. Here they offered two medals, one for an *awdl* on 'Ystyriaeth ar Oes Dyn' [The Life of Man], and the other for the best penillion singer with the harp.

(William Davies Leathart, *The Origin and Progress of the Gwyneddigion Society of London*, London, 1831.)

E.7   *Saturday, Sept. 21* (1792). This being the day on which the autumnal equinox occurred, some Welsh Bards, resident in London, assembled in congress on Primrose Hill, according to ancient usage, . . . The wonted ceremonies were observed. A circle of stones formed, in the middle of which was the *Maen Gorsedd*, or altar, on which a naked sword being placed, all the Bards assisted to sheathe it. This ceremony was attended with a proclamation, the substance of which was, that the Bards of the Island of Britain (for such is their antient title) were the heralds and ministers of peace . . . On this occasion the Bards appeared in the insignia of their various orders. The presiding Bards were David Samwell, of the primitive, and claimant of the ovation order; William Owen, of the ovation and primitive orders; Edward Jones, of the ovation, and claimant of the primitive order; and *Edward Williams*, of the primitive and druidic orders. The Bardic traditions, and several odes, were recited. Two of the odes, one by David Samwell, on the Bardic discipline, the other by *Edward Williams*, on the Bardic mythology, were in English; and the first that were ever in the language recited at a congress of Ancient British Bards. This was with an intention to give the English reader an idea of what, though very common in Wales, has never yet been properly known in England. The

Bardic Institution of the Ancient Britains, which is the same as the Druidic, has been from the earliest times, through all ages, to the present day, retained by the Welsh . . . [and] is now exactly the same that it was two thousand years ago . . .

(Iolo Morganwg's letter to *The Gentleman's Magazine*, 1792, LXII, pp.956–7.)

E.8 I perfectly agree with you in your Sentiments of Mr Owen's *Bardism*. It is a *made Dish*, cooked up from obscure scraps of the ancient Bards, and the Cabala [the pretended arcana] of the modern ones; a superficial acquaintance with the Metempsychosis; and these ingredients spiced with an immoderate quantity of wild Invention.

(Letters of Edward Davies, Cardiff Central Library, MS 3, Collection 104, Vol.VI, letter 3.)

E.9 As we, the Remains of the British Nation, who have sole Interest in the honour of this antient Celtick Tongue, are forever obliged to that great Light of our British Antiquities, the learned Pezron, for his extraordinary Pains and Industry . . . so we ought to be no less grateful to the Memory of the late exquisitely learn'd and judicious Mr *Edward Lhwyd* . . . These two now mentioned Gentlemen, having by different Methods open'd a Way of resolving diverse Tongues in Europe, to one Mother-Language, which language indeed Mr *Lhwyd* leaves modestly undecided, but by Monsieur Pezron is determin'd to be the Celtick . . .

(Henry Rowlands, *Mona Antiqua Restaurata*, Dublin, 1723, pp.316–17.)

E.10 They [the Druids] had their groves, the till then inseparable concomitants of the Druidish priesthood, which the sacrilegious Romans immediately cut down and demolished. And to this day here are places retaining the ancient name of *Llwynau* or groves, as *Llwyn Llwyd*, *Llwyn Moel*, *Llwyn On*, *Llwyn Ogan*, and *Llwyn y Coed*, in or near every one of which may be remarked some remains of Druidish worship; either broken altars, pillars, or remains of a *Carnedd*. And no doubt there were many more groves, whose names are lost and quite forgotten.

It being now made somewhat apparent on the evidence produced, that the Chief Druidical residence was in the Isle of Mona, and particularly in and about the place now called Llanidan parish; it may then be expected that that place of all the island, must be at that time most plentifully adorned with a variety of formed groves, containing in them mounts, pillars, heaps, altars, and other appurtenances of their superstitious worship. And that although the groves surrounding them be now quite gone and perished, and the ancient names of them be utterly lost, yet it may be justly expected that many of the more lasting erections (on the supposal I offer) should remain there, as standing monuments of their long forgotten superannuated uses. And indeed in that respect there are of such enough to answer the end, and to give sufficient satisfaction to a just and reasonable enquirer.

(Henry Rowlands, *Mona Antiqua Restaurata*, 2nd ed., London, 1766, p.87.)

E.11   I now enter on classical ground, and the pious seats of the antient *Druids*; the sacred groves, the altars, and monumental stones. A slight mention of what I saw must content my reader; who is referred to the works of the celebrated and learned Mr Henry Rowlands, the former vicar of this place [Llanidan].

(Thomas Pennant, *A Tour in Wales*, MDCCLXX, London, 1783, II, p.229.)

E.12   Thursday, December 2 1802. We left Capel Cerig early this morning on horseback with the design of examining the Celtic remains in the Isle of Anglesea the Harper of the inn accompanying us in the capacity of interpreter.

(Revd John Skinner, 'Ten Days' Tour through the Isle of Anglesea', *Archaeologia Cambrensis Supplement*, 1908, p.9.)

E.13   In the parish of Nolton is a village called Drewson, corruptly for Druidstown, near which on the road leading from Fishguard to Dale there occurs a remarkable inclosure, occupying near an acre of ground, called Drewson chapel. The stones that composed the druidical circle were removed in 1740 to build with, so that there is scarce any thing left to mark the situation of the spacious *Gorsedd*, or place of convention for various purposes.

(Richard Fenton, *A Historical Tour Through Pembrokeshire*, London, 1811, p.157.)

E.14   On a rock, whose haughty brow
Frowns o'er old Conway's foaming flood,
Robed in the sable garb of woe
With haggard eyes the Poet stood;
(Loose his beard and hoary hair
Steam'd like a meteor to the troubled air)
And with a master's hand and prophet's fire
Struck the deep sorrows of his lyre:
'Hark, how each giant oak and desert cave
Sighs to the torrent's awful voice beneath!
O'er thee, O King! their hundred arms they wave,
Revenge on thee in hoarser murmurs breathe:
Vocal no more, since Cambria's fatal day,
To high-born Hoel's harp, or soft Llewellyn's lay.

(The second verse of Thomas Gray's ode, 'The Bard', 1757.)

E.15   The Welsh have a tradition, that these uncouth and savage mountains [of Snowdonia] formerly abounded with woods, and that they were felled by *Edward I* . . . There may be more truth in another tradition, that this king ordered all the bards of Wales to be destroyed. It was a necessary policy, without which, he could not secure his new conquest. By these means, he eradicated the first principles of resistance, which always arose from the inflammatory and prophetical songs of those turbulent and enthusiastic poetasters. If some should regret the poems, existence of which the massacre obstructed, they may find some comfort on the reflection, that, it has given birth to one of the finest odes in the English tongue [Gray's ode].

(Henry Penruddocke Wyndham, *A Tour Through Monmouthshire and Wales, made in . . . 1774 & 1777*, 2nd ed., 1781, pp.148–9.)

E.16 Having washed and taken tea we roamed out in the village [of Beddgelert], a very pretty romantic place at the foot of Snowdon. It takes its name from Gelert, the greyhound, *Bethgelert the grave of Gelert*. The story of the hound destroying a wolf that came in to a cottage whilst human assistance was absent and saving the life of Prince Llewellyn's child and afterward being slain by the Prince who supposed too hastily the dog had killed his son, is known to everyone. The poor dog's grave is in a field by the Church and marked by a large stone and the Master of the Inn where we put up has a fine large greyhound in memory of the event which is honoured by the name of Gelert.

(Dafydd Tomos (ed.), *Michael Faraday in Wales*, Gwasg Gee, n.d., p.75.)

E.17 Not having an opportunity of coming to the Society to- night, I thought it would be agreeable to the members to be informed that Gwilym Owain [William Owen Pughe] and myself had an audience with General Bowles [a Cherokee Chief] this morning and that his information places the existence of a race of Welsh Indians beyond all manner of doubt however extra-ordinary it may appear in the History of our Country, I am now clearly convinced of its being a fact. Genl. Bowles describes them as very numerous and the most warlike nation on the American Continent. They are situated on the river Missouri exactly as they are laid down in the best Maps under the name of Padougas, by which it is clear that they have preserved the name of *Madog* to this day. He supposes that they landed about the mouth of the river Mississippi. He says that they have books among them tho' they can't read them. A Welshman not long ago passed through the middle of their country who escaped from the Mines of Mexico whom he thinks is the only white man who has been among them for a great length of time. They keep unmixed in general, are different in complexion from the Aboriginal Inhabitants, and many of them have Red Hair. He has not been in the country himself, but has been on the borders.

The Bard by Philippe J. de Loutherbourg, published in 1784 as the frontispiece to *Musical and Poetical Relicks of the Welsh Bards* by Edward Jones.

His people the Creeks know them very well, it will not be a difficult matter for anyone to get into their country.

(David Samwell's letter to the Gwyneddigion Society, 23 March 1791. British Museum Add. MS 14957.)

E.18   Mr E. Williams [*Iolo Morganwg*] and myself have collected a great deal of information lately. About six weeks ago we had interviews with two merchants one living in New Orleans at the mouth of the Mississippi, and the other at St Louis, a little above the junction of the Missouri and the Mississippi. They have had continual accounts of the Madogion for many years which put the truth of their existence to those gentlemen beyond all doubt, and all agree of their being in a state of considerable civilization compared with the Indians . . . Mr E. Williams has made a collection of all the material accounts between 30 & 40 in number respecting the Welsh Indians . . . A great many Gentlemen are willing to subscribe to support people going over . . . Mr E. Williams and a young man from Caernarvonshire [John Evans] will set off towards the latter end of the year, whether they meet with encouragement or not.

(William Owen Pughe's letter to Paul Panton of Plas Gwyn, May 1792. National Library of Wales MS 9072E.)

E.19   The Revd William Gilpin's description of the town of Brecon:
        Brecknoc is a very romantic place, abounding with broken grounds, torrents, dismantled towers, and ruins of every kind. I have seen few places, where a landscape-painter might get a collection of better ideas.

Gilpin's description of Dinefwr Castle, Carmarthenshire:
        The woods, which adorn these beautiful scenes about Dinevawr-castle, and which are clumped with great beauty, consist chiefly of the finest oak . . .
        The picturesque scenes, which this place affords, are numerous. Wherever the castle appears, and it appears almost every where, a landscape of purely picturesque is generally presented. The ground is so beautifully disposed, that it is almost impossible to have bad composition. And the opposite

side of the vale often appears as a back-ground; and makes a pleasing distance.

(Revd William Gilpin, *Observations on the River Wye, and Several Parts of South Wales, &c. Relative Chiefly to Picturesque Beauty; made in the Summer of the Year 1770*, London, 1782, pp. 51 and 63.)

E.20   Daniel Defoe's observations on the Welsh landscape in 1726, which are in complete contrast to the opinions of the romantic travellers of the late eighteenth century, such as William Gilpin:

Brecknockshire is a mere inland county, as Radnor is; the English jestingly (and I think not very improperly) call it Breakneckshire. 'Tis mountainous to an extremity . . . Entering this shire [Glamorgan], from Radnor and Brecknock, we were saluted with Monuchdenny-Hill on our left, and the Black-Mountain on the right, and all a ridge of horrid rocks and precipices between, over which, if we had not had trusty guides, we should never have found our way; and indeed, we began to repent our curiosity, as not having met with any thing worth the trouble; and a country looking so full of horror, that we thought to have given over the enterprise, and have left Wales out of our circuit.

(Pat Rogers (ed.), *Daniel Defoe: A Tour through the Whole Island of Great Britain, 1724–26*, 1971, pp.376–7.)

Debating the Evidence

This chapter is concerned with ideas about Wales. To a remarkable degree these ideas were mistaken — even bogus — but the important thing about them is that they were held or believed by intelligent contemporaries, however improbable or even absurd they may seem to us. The interesting selection of extracts from letters, topographical works and other sources shows above all a growing consciousness of Wales and things Welsh; they illustrate some of the reasons for this. Most of the documents are primary sources for the history of ideas, especially ideas about the Welsh past; they tell us little about the realities of eighteenth-century Wales.

Source E.1

The Cambrian Register was one of the several efforts made by London Welshmen from 1789 into the early years of the nineteenth century to edit and publish scholarly material relating to the Welsh past, and especially texts of Welsh literature. Why might London Welshmen have been so prominent in producing material of this kind?

Source E.2

This letter was written in 1758 by *Lewis Morris* to Edward Richard, the schoolmaster of Ystradmeurig, whose pupil *Evan Evans* had been, excitedly informing him of the discovery of the Book of Aneurin, containing the very early poem, *Y Gododdin*. The riches of Welsh poetry were only gradually revealed to the public in the eighteenth century, since up until that time virtually everything that survived had been preserved in manuscripts in private hands.

Source E.3

Stung by the doubts expressed by English authors that early Welsh literature did not exist, *Iolo Morganwg* set about adding to the corpus which had survived. Many of his texts were long accepted as genuine. What difficulties might historians have in dealing with fabrications of this kind?

Sources E.1, E.2 and E.3

On the face of it there is little discernible difference between the views expressed by William Owen Pughe, *Lewis Morris*, *Evan Evans* (Ieuan Fardd) and *Iolo Morganwg* in these three extracts. But, in the light of what Paul Evans says in his introductory essay, how does *Iolo Morganwg* differ from the others?

Source E.4

The annual almanacs were among the few vehicles for the publication of secular Welsh verse (both ancient and contemporary) in the eighteenth century. Siôn Rhydderch was an important publisher of Welsh books at Shrewsbury, and he was the compiler of a Welsh grammar and dictionary, as well as being a minor poet and frequenter of *eisteddfodau*.

Source E.5

Jonathan Hughes of Llangollen (1721–1805) was a very productive

Druidical Remains in Anglesey, an engraving by J. Smith in William Sotheby's *A Tour Through Parts of Wales*, 1794.

country poet who competed in the *eisteddfodau* of the *Gwyneddigion*. His letter indicates the poverty of the Welsh poets deprived of the traditional patronage of the gentry and in great need of encouragement and patronage from the comparatively wealthy London Welsh.

Source E.6
Alone of these extracts this one cannot be regarded as a primary source. Why is this?

Sources E.4, E.5 and E.6
On the basis of these sources, what kind of gatherings were the eighteenth-century *eisteddfodau*?

Source E.7
The Gentleman's Magazine was a very reputable monthly journal published in London. *Iolo Morganwg* had often had letters and articles published in it, and here he uses it to publicize the sensational meeting of the *Gorsedd* of Bards on Primrose Hill, London, at the autumnal equinox of 1792. This report could be taken as a primary source for what happened on this occasion, but the unscrupulous Iolo gives a totally misleading account of its meaning, significance and antiquity. It was in fact the first ever meeting of the *Gorsedd*!

Source E.8
John Walters (1721–97) had known *Iolo Morganwg* very well for many years and he was a good enough Welsh scholar not to be taken in by the latter's ideas about bardism and druidism. Contrast Sources E.7 and E.8. But which view prevailed?

Sources E.9 and E.10
Although his *Gorsedd* was bogus, *Iolo Morganwg* was doing no more than adding further details to a large and elaborate body of beliefs about the antiquity of the Welsh language and, more especially, about the druids, which pervaded antiquarian thought in the eighteenth century. Henry Rowlands, an Anglesey parson, was one of those who helped to propagate such ideas about the remote past of Wales. Sources E.7–E.15 give us various accounts of druids and bards; do they show that native Welsh scholars were as obsessed with druidism as were English poets and tourists?

Sources E.11 — E.15

What can be deduced from these documents about the reasons why significant numbers of gentlemen began to tour Wales towards the end of the eighteenth century?

Source E.16

This document vividly illustrates the dangers of accepting popular history as true. The story of Gelert, as Paul Evans shows, is not even a 'genuine' legend.

Sources E.17 and E.18

Why were the 'Welsh Indians' so important to the *Gwyneddigion* and other London Welshmen in the 1790s? (Read also Gwyn A. Williams's chapter 'Beginnings of Radicalism' before considering this.)

Source E.19

Compare this with Sources E.11–E.15. Does Gilpin present a further reason for visiting Wales in the late eighteenth century?

Sources E.19 and E.20

Contrast Defoe's and Gilpin's responses to the Welsh landscape.

Discussion

In contrast to the other chapters in this book the majority (in fact 70 per cent) of the sources of this chapter come from books and magazines printed between 1723 and 1831. Several of the extracts are scholarly manifestos connected with the heroic efforts to get Welsh literary manuscripts into print, others are accounts of tours in Wales in search of picturesque scenery and the romantic remains of the druidic past. The most influential and distinguished work of literature quoted is *Thomas Gray*'s 'The Bard' (Source E.14) which is in many ways symbolic of a new interest in things Welsh detectable among the English reading public in the second half of the eighteenth century. As primary sources for the historian, these works have a particular function. The extracts quoted here are used to uncover attitudes towards the Welsh past, not a past carefully reconstructed from the documentary and archaeological evidence (Sir John Lloyd's *History of Wales from the Earliest Times to the*

Edwardian Conquest, published in 1911, was really the first sustained history of this kind) but one based on a curious vision peopled by druids and bards.

Central to this version is the contribution of *Edward Williams, Iolo Morganwg* (1747–1826), the Glamorgan stonemason-scholar. He was a true scholar, but one in whom the intoxicating combination of romanticism and *laudanum* produced distortions of reality and actual forgery of historical documents and literary texts. He was more, too, as reading through this book will reveal — extracts from Iolo's voluminous writings provide no fewer than seven sources (A.27, E.3, E.7, C.2, D.2, D.4 and D.10). From only one chapter is he absent — 'The New Enthusiasts' — and even there Geraint Jenkins could have quoted him — had he chosen to do so — as one of the most outspoken critics of *Methodism. Iolo Morganwg* thus bestrides the whole range of Welsh affairs, cultural, religious, political and even economic. This shows him as something of a polymath, but, even more significantly, it exemplifies the 'seamless web' (F.W. Maitland, 1850–1906) of history. Historians have tended to compartmentalize aspects of the past, but the whole could be comprehended within the mind of one exceptional individual.

In an especially profound way *Iolo Morganwg* combined a romantic vision of Welsh history and literature with a radical view of contemporary politics and religion to create a new concept of a Welsh nation. 'What Iolo was offering the Welsh was a revival of ancient traditions which in fact constituted a new, and radical, national ideology', wrote Gwyn A. Williams in *Madoc: the Making of a Myth* (p.105).

Further Reading

Evans, E.D., *A History of Wales 1660–1815*, Cardiff, 1979.

Howell, David, *Patriarchs and Parasites: The Gentry of South-West Wales in the Eighteenth Century*, Cardiff, 1987.

Jenkins, Geraint H., *The Foundations of Modern Wales: Wales 1642–1780*, Cardiff/Oxford, 1987.

Jenkins, Geraint H., *Hanes Cymru yn y Cyfnod Modern Cynnar, 1530–1760*, Caerdydd, 1983.

Jenkins, Geraint H., *Literature, Religion and Society in Wales, 1660–1730*, Cardiff, 1978.

Jenkins, Philip, *The Making of a Ruling Class: The Glamorgan Gentry 1640–1790*, Cambridge, 1983.

Jenkins, R.T., *Hanes Cymru yn y Ddeunawfed Ganrif*, Caerdydd, 1928.

Jones, D.J.V., *Before Rebecca*, London, 1973.

Moore, Donald (ed.), *Wales in the Eighteenth Century*, Swansea, 1976.

Morgan, Prys T.J., *Iolo Morganwg*, Cardiff, 1975.

Morgan, Prys T.J., *The Eighteenth Century Renaissance*, Llandybïe, 1981.

Parry, Thomas, *A History of Welsh Literature*, Oxford, 1955.

Rees, William, *Industry before the Industrial Revolution*, 2 vols., Cardiff, 1968.

Roberts, R.O., 'The Development and Decline of the Non-Ferrous Metal Smelting Industries in South Wales', *Transactions of the Honourable Society of Cymmrodorion*, 1956.

Thomas, P.D.G., 'Jacobitism in Wales', *Welsh History Review*, I, 1962.

Williams, Gwyn A., *Madoc: The Making of a Myth*, London, 1979.

Williams, Gwyn A., *The Search for Beulah Land*, London, 1980.

Glossary

Aeneid	Poem by the Latin author Virgil (70–19 BC) relating the story of Aeneas of Troy.
Anabaptists	See *Baptists*.
Aneirin	Supposed author of the early Welsh poem, *The Gododdin*, which relates the story of a disastrous battle against the Anglians at Catterick, *c*.AD 600.
Anticlericalism	Opposition to the power and influence of the clergy or the Church in secular affairs.
ap Gwilym, Dafydd	See *Dafydd ap Gwilym*.
Arianism	Doctrine denying the true divinity of Christ, who is seen as one of God's creatures endowed with divinity by the Father, and not as a co-equal member of the Trinity.
Armiger	Esquire (literally, one who bears arms).
Arminians	Those who hold the doctrine of general redemption, in opposition to *Calvinists* who believe that only the elect will be saved.
Atterbury Plot	Jacobite plot named from Francis Atterbury, Bishop of Rochester (1662–1732).
Awdl	Long poem in the strict metres, for which the chair is awarded at the National *Eisteddfod*.
Baptists	Dissenting denomination distinguished from the

Independents by the practice of believers' baptism; often termed Anabaptists by their opponents.

Beaumarchais, Pierre-Augustin Caron de	(1732–99) French dramatist, creator of the character Figaro.
Bedlam	Bethlehem Hospital for the insane, London.
Bendigedig, rhowch foliant	Literally, Blessed, give praise.
Bevan, Bridget	(1698–1779) Supporter of Griffith Jones's *circulating schools*, especially after his death in 1761; known as 'Madam Bevan'.
Blake, William	(1757–1827) English poet and artist.
Burgesses	Leading citizens of a chartered borough; in most Welsh boroughs they possessed a parliamentary vote.
Burke, Edmund	(1729–97) Irish politician and philosopher, author of *Reflections on the French Revolution*.
Calamy, Edmund	(1671–1732) English biographer of the Nonconformist ministers ejected in 1660–2.
Calvinists	Followers of the distinctive doctrine of Jean Calvin of Geneva that only the elect will be saved (see also *Arminians*). The Welsh *Methodists* were Calvinists.
Catechism	A set of questions and answers on the principal points of the Christian faith, printed as part of the Anglican *Book of Common Prayer*, with many later versions by Dissenters and others.
Catholics	Term exclusively used in the eighteenth century of the adherents of the Roman Catholic church; otherwise referred to as papists.
Charles, Thomas	(1755–1814) Leading Welsh *Methodist* of the late eighteenth and early nineteenth centuries, especially famous for organizing Sunday schools.
Chartists	Advocates of the 'Charter', the programme of the

parliamentary reform movement, prominent during the years 1837–48.

Chartist march on Newport Rising in the western valleys of Monmouthshire (Gwent) defeated by troops at Newport in 1839.

Circulating schools System of elementary education founded by Griffith Jones (1683–1761), rector of Llanddowror, Carmarthenshire (Dyfed).

Civil War The war between King Charles I and Parliament, 1642–5.

Congregationalists See *Independents*.

County Bench Commonly used collective term for the magistrates or *justices of the peace* for a county.

Cromlechs Prehistoric stone monuments (now termed megaliths), in the eighteenth century believed to have been built by the Druids.

Cromwell, Oliver (1599–1658) General of the New Model Army in the *Civil War* and subsequently Lord Protector of England.

Culm Anthracite coal dust or small coal.

Cylchgrawn Periodical or magazine.

Dafydd ap Gwilym (*fl.*1315–50) The greatest of the medieval Welsh poets.

Deists Believers in the existence of a god, but who denied the revealed religion of Christianity.

Deputy-lieutenant Leading gentleman of a county, one of those having certain military and other functions under the Lord Lieutenant.

Despard Conspiracy Attempted *coup d'etat* in 1802 led by Colonel Edward Marcus Despard (1751–1803).

Dissent Nonconformity — conscientious refusal to accept the doctrines, ceremonies and order of the Church of England.

Edward I King of England 1272–1307; conquered the principality of Gwynedd in 1282.

Eisteddfod A meeting of bards.

Enclosures The fencing of common land (in Wales, mostly upland grazings) for use by individual farmers.

Enlightenment Eighteenth-century philosophical movement stressing the importance of reason as against received authority and tradition, especially in religious matters. The century is often called the 'Age of Reason'.

Evans, Revd Evan (1731–88) Important Welsh poet and scholar, known as Ieuan Fardd or Ieuan Brydydd Hir.

Evans, Theophilus (1693–1767) Author of a Welsh prose classic, *Drych y Prif Oesoedd* (1716), and strong opponent of *Methodism*.

Freeholders Landowners; freeholders with property worth more than 40 shillings a year had the parliamentary vote in county constituencies.

Freemasonry Fraternity or secret society, originating in the medieval guilds of stonemasons.

French Revolution Revolution beginning with the fall of the Bastille in 1789. It introduced democracy and abolished monarchy.

George of Hanover Protestant German prince who succeeded the childless Queen Anne as King George I in 1714.

Glan-y-gors, Jac John Jones (1766–1821), satirical poet living in London; published the views of Tom Paine in *Seren tan Gwmwl* (1795) and *Toriad y Dydd* (1797).

Goethe, Johann Wolfgang von (1749–1832) German poet.

Gorsedd Bardic organization and ceremonial invented by *Iolo Morganwg* in the 1790s.

Gray, Thomas (1716–71) English poet.

Gwladfa Colony or national home for the Welsh in America.

Gwyneddigion Literary and cultural society of the London Welsh, founded in 1770. It promoted *eisteddfodau* and the publication of Welsh manuscripts.

Habeas corpus	Writ requiring a person to be brought into court following his or her arrest, i.e. limiting the authorities' power to detain a suspect without a formal charge being brought. Habeas corpus was suspended from 1794 to 1801 during the war against Revolutionary France.
Iliad	The great poem by the Greek poet Homer, relating the story of the siege of Troy.
Independents	Dissenting sect whose distinctive doctrine is the independence (under God) of the local congregation — hence also Congregationalists.
Iolo Morganwg	Edward Williams (1747–1826). Stonemason, polymath and democrat — also literary forger and inventor of the *Gorsedd*.
Jacobite	Sympathizer with or follower of the deposed King James II and his dynasty.
James III	Son of James II, recognized as James III by the Catholic powers, but usually known in Britain as the 'Pretender', or the 'Old Pretender' to distinguish him from his son. Led the 1715 rebellion against George I.
Jones, Thomas (of Pencerrig)	(1742–1803) Landscape painter and Radnorshire squire.
Jones, Thomas	(1756–1820) Calvinistic Methodist minister.
Jones, William (of Llangadfan)	(1726–95) Poet and *Voltairean* radical.
Justice of the peace	Magistrate; gentleman exercising wide administrative and judicial powers in a county under commission from the Crown.
Knights	Knights of the shire — members of Parliament for county constituencies.
Laudanum	Tincture of opium.
Laudian High Churchmen	Anglicans following the example of Archbishop Laud (1573–1645) who emphasized the Catholic inheritance

of the Church of England in opposition to the *Puritans*.

Les Ruines	See *Volney*.
Lhuyd, Edward	Welsh scholar and keeper of the Ashmolean Museum, Oxford.
Lieutenancy	Collective term for the *deputy-lieutenants* of a county.
Llywarch Hen	Early Welsh hero, to whom a series of poems written in the ninth and tenth centuries was attributed.
Llywelyn the Great	(1173–1240) Llywelyn ap Iorwerth, Prince of Gwynedd.
Louis XIV	(1638–1715) King of France 1643–1715.
Loutherbourg, Philippe de	(1740–1812) German landscape artist.
Mackworths	Family of landowners living at Neath in west Glamorgan. The first member of the family to settle in Wales was Sir Humphrey Mackworth (1657–1727), industrialist and founder of the SPCK.
Madoc	Son of the Welsh prince Owain Gwynedd. He was said to have discovered America in the twelfth century and to have been the ancestor of a tribe of Welsh-speaking Indians, thought in the late eighteenth century to be living in the Midwest.
Magnate	Wealthy landowner, usually a peer.
Mansell, Robert	(1695–1723) Eldest son of the first Lord Mansell of Margam; considered to have been a *Jacobite*.
Mass	A title for the central rite of the Christian religion — the Eucharist, Holy Communion or Lord's Supper. Especially applies to the Roman Catholic church.
Maugre	In spite of (arch).
Megaliths	See *Cromlechs*.
Methodism	Revival movement in the Church of England beginning in the 1730s and eventually breaking away to form a Nonconformist denomination.

Morganwg, Iolo See *Iolo Morganwg*.

Morris Letters Letters of the Morris brothers of Anglesey (Lewis, Richard, William and John), known as 'Morrisiaid Môn'.

Morris, Lewis (1701–65) Poet, antiquary and surveyor; one of the Morris brothers of Anglesey.

Navy Act Act of 1795 for the raising of men for the Navy.

Out-boroughs Boroughs which joined with the county town to elect a member of Parliament.

Papists See *Catholics*.

Paradise Lost Epic poem by John Milton (1608–74) on the fall of man, published in 1667.

Peace of Amiens Peace between Britain and France, March 1802 to May 1803.

Penillion Literally verses, but often a technical term applied to a contrapuntal and extempore form of singing to the harp.

Pennant, Thomas (1726–98) Naturalist and antiquary; lived at Downing, Flintshire (Clwyd).

Philipps, Sir John (c.1666–1737) Influential member of the SPCK and patron of Griffith Jones of Llanddowror; lived at Picton Castle, Pembrokeshire (Dyfed).

Powell, Vavasor (1617–70) Puritan preacher and writer.

Presbyterians Dissenting denomination believing in form of church government by presbyters and synods; in Wales almost indistinguishable from the *Independents*.

Presbyterian-Unitarian In the second half of the eighteenth century most *Presbyterians* in Wales were moving along the theological spectrum from *Arminianism* through *Arianism* to *Socinianism* and *Unitarianism*.

Pretender See *James III*.

Price, Richard (1723–91) Dissenting minister and philosopher who welcomed the American and French revolutions.

Priestley, Dr Joseph	(1733–1804) *Unitarian* minister, scientist and radical.
Proletariat	Social class owning no property, and so dependent upon wage-earning.
Puddling process	Process of converting pig iron to wrought or bar iron, invented by Henry Cort and widely adopted in south Wales in the 1790s.
Puritans	Strict Protestants who wished to purify the Church of England of its Catholic features.
Quorum	Originally, certain especially well-qualified *justices of the peace* whose presence was necessary at a meeting of the quarter sessions, etc. By the eighteenth century all justices were named of the quorum.
Rebecca Riots	Agrarian disturbances in west Wales, 1839–43, featuring attacks on toll-gates led by a man in woman's clothes ('Rebecca').
Recte	Rightly, correctly.
Recusants	Catholics who refused to attend Church of England services.
Reformation	Movement for the reform of the Church which brought in Protestantism, the rejection of the authority of the Pope, and the dissolution of the monasteries in the sixteenth century.
Restoration	Restoration of the monarchy in 1660 after the Commonwealth.
Reverberatory furnace	Furnace in which metal is smelted by an indirect heat.
Rhowch foliant/ Rhowch glod	Literally, give praise.
Roman Catholics	See *Catholics*.
Roundheads	Supporters of Parliament in the *Civil War*.
Ruins	See *Volney*.

Sandby, Paul	(1725–1809) English watercolourist and engraver.
Sansculottes	Literally, without knee-breeches. Term applied to ultra-democrats of the *French Revolution*, especially to poor, ill-clad leaders of the populace.
Sheriffs	Chief officers of counties, appointed annually by the Crown, with responsibility for (*inter alia*) law enforcement and conducting elections.
Shrewsbury Drapers	Merchants at Shrewsbury who dominated much of the trade in Welsh cloth.
Socinianism	Derived from the names of two continental theologians who held *Unitarian* views.
Stukeley, William	(1687–1765) English antiquary, especially interested in Druidism.
Taliesin	Sixth-century poet, the author of a number of poems contained in the fourteenth-century *Book of Taliesin*.
Tory	Name first applied to a political party in the reign of Charles II; the party were in favour of the royal prerogative, hereditary succession to the crown and the privileges of the Church, and were opposed to religious toleration. They were excluded from office after 1714.
Transubstantiation	Transformation of the substance of the bread and wine of the Eucharist into the body and blood of Christ; a doctrine denied by Protestant churches.
Treason trials	Trials of leading English democrats suspected of spreading the ideas of the *French Revolution*, 1794.
Unitarian	Dissenter rejecting the orthodox doctrine of the Trinity and, thus, denying the divinity of Christ.
Volney, Constantin de	(1757–1820) French aristocrat, author of *Les Ruines, ou Méditations sur les Revolutions des Empires* (1791), a work advocating equality of all men, the overthrow of despotism, and religious toleration.
Voltairean	Follower of the doctrines of the French philosopher,

	Voltaire (1694–1778), one of the great figures of the *Enlightenment*.
Weald	Wooded region of Kent and Sussex famous for its charcoal iron industry.
Weighs	See *Wey*.
Werther	*Die Leiden des jungen Werthers*, immensely popular and influential novel by *Goethe* published in 1774.
Wesley, John	(1703–91) Leader of the *Arminian* or Wesleyan *Methodists*.
Wey (Weigh)	Measure of coal, equal to about eight tons.
Whig	Political party, first named in the reign of Charles II, upholding parliamentary supremacy and religious toleration. The Glorious Revolution of 1688 and the Protestant Succession of 1714 were their triumphs and they largely dominated the government after 1714.
Wilkes, John	(1727–97) Radical English politician and journalist, arrested by a general warrant for seditious libel in 1763. His case established the important principle that general warrants are illegal.
Williams, David	(1738–1816) Radical political writer and *Deist*, a native of the Caerphilly area of mid-Glamorgan.
Williams, Edward	See *Iolo Morganwg*.

Index

Index

Index